D1476610

EARLY LIGHTING — A Pictorial Guide

EARLY LIGHTING

A PICTORIAL GUIDE

Compiled and Published by The Rushlight Club

Printed in the United States of America by
Finlay Brothers, Inc., Hartford, Connecicut 06106

Binding by Stanhope Bindery, Inc., Boston, Massachusetts

Foreword

We are fascinated today by the antiquity of man, by his sociological development and by his technological advancement. An important contributor to this progress has been the development of lighting which extends both his leisure and working hours and adds to his comfort and security.

The Rushlight Club, founded in Boston in November 1932, is one of the oldest organizations dedicated to the study of one phase of antiquity. It began as a few collectors met socially in each other's homes to discuss new acquisitions of early lighting devices and to exchange information on research of the subject. It adopted for its emblem the rushlight holder, a primitive iron device used to support the frugal but efficient burning rush.

The purpose of the Club as set forth by its founders, and which remains unchanged today, is to: "stimulate an interest in the study of early lighting including the use of early lighting devices and lighting fluids, and the origin and development of each, by means of written articles, lectures, conferences, exhibitions from private collections, and if desired through the medium of exchange; and its object shall be to collect, preserve, and disseminate information and data obtained through these studies."

We are indebted to the founders, as well as those who have followed, who have kept this purpose in mind and have developed, added to, and refined the stature of lighting information through study and research. Today, as an international organization, over 300 members carry on this tradition.

Since the Club's organization, a quarterly bulletin, "The Rushlight", has been published treating all phases of early lighting. The Club has also participated in the publication of two well known reference books, "Flickering Flames", an original work by one of the charter members, Leroy L. Thwing, and "Old Lamps of Central Europe", a partial translation from the German by Mr. Thwing, from the original "Das Beleuchtungswesen" by Ladislaus Von Benesch.

It was felt that a pictorial reference which would bring together many examples of all types of early lighting devices, arranged in order of their historical appearance, would be invaluable to students and collectors. The Club's archives contain a wealth of photographs taken of lamps which members have brought to meetings for discussion. A Publication Committee composed of Mr. and Mrs. Lawrence S. Cooke, Mr. and Mrs. Harry W. Rapp Jr., and Mr. and Mrs. George H. Sherwood undertook the selection of representative examples of lighting devices from the archives and other photographs taken during visits to the homes of members. Information on each device was obtained from the owner or gleaned from reference material to provide written descriptions to accompany the pictures.

The Committee would be remiss if it did not recognize and express appreciation to the many members who have generously given of resources, knowledge, time, as well as made their collections available to complete this work.

Every effort has been made to provide accurate and succinct information to accomplish the objectives of this book — a complete and quick reference guide to all phases of early lighting. It is our sincere desire that this has been accomplished.

November 1972
Rushlight Club Fortieth Anniversary

Harry W. Rapp Jr.
President

ACKNOWLEDGEMENTS

This publication has been made possible through the generosity of the following members who have made their collections available for photographing and provided background information:

Preston R. Bassett, Abraham Brooks, Mrs. G. W. Bryant, C. Fred Burdett, Mrs. Robert W. Cole, Lawrence S. Cooke, Quentin L. Coons, Julius Daniels, Oliver W. Deming, Mrs. Frank H. Dillaby, Edward Durell, Mrs. Cy Gold, Wm. A. Harriman, Frederick L. Hodes, James A. Keillor, Mrs. Amos C. Kingsbury, Paul Ladd, Bertram K. Little, John Mack*, Charles J. McCabe*, William A. O'Connell, George O'Connor, Ronald W. Olmstead, Mrs. Albert N. Peterson, Douglas W. Rapp, Harry W. Rapp Jr., Edwin B. Rollins, George H. Sherwood, Howard W. Stone*, Mrs. Lura Woodside Watkins, C. Malcolm Watkins, John H. Witham, Miss Rhoda Ziegler, and subscribing institutions Old Sturbridge Village, Smithsonian Institution.

*Deceased

CONTENTS

INTRODUCTION

For the beginning collector of antiques, as well as the serious student, there are excellent periodicals and books of reference to which he can go for instruction and identification, with the exception, however, of the student of early lighting.

For the lighting collector, aside from texts dealing with history and development, there is no single source to which he can turn for quick identification of lighting devices in his collection. This book is intended to supply that want so far as possible.

On the pages that follow there are assembled, in effect, a graphic museum of early lighting devices and accessories. The contents have been chosen to illustrate the scope of items that might be encountered by the collector. The limited text is intended to serve as a museum guide pointing out distinguishing features that may or may not be typical.

The chapters have been arranged so far as possible according to the chronological order of the fuels and the technology involved. Specialized lights, devices for creating fire, and accessories, often a part of lighting collections, are included. Not included, however, are the centrally served lighting systems of gas and electricity.

The two main objectives have been to provide an easy source of identification and an evolutionary organization of material that would be of value to the lighting collector, and at the same time add interest in the lighting items often found in various nonlighting collections.

Although much of the information has been borrowed from the pages of *The Rushlight,* with few exceptions the illustrations are new and have never before appeared in print.

In the descriptive data, dimensions, materials and markings were accurately taken from the items themselves but in some cases the owner's best belief was relied upon for dating and provenance.

The intentionally brief comments accompanying the illustrations will, it is hoped, whet the appetite of the serious collector or student for further study. To this end, the bibliography on page 125 should prove helpful. Listed are only publications devoted solely to lighting, some of which are general in nature while others are highly specialized. Ten of the books indicated (†) which are readily available together with *The Rushlight* (available to members only) would constitute a basic library for the serious collector.

Not listed in the bibliography are many valuable sources that contain occasional references to lighting.

Among periodicals, *The Scientific American* for the last half of the nineteenth century is a rich source of general lighting information and includes such material on safety as well as patents.

The United States *Patent Office Reports,* 1848-1871, followed by the United States *Patent Office Gazettes,* as well as the *Journal of the Franklin Institute,* Philadelphia, 1826 — and Silliman's *American Journal of Science and Arts,* New York 1818 —, document the progress of lighting technology.

Collectors' periodicals such as *Antiques, Hobbies,* etc., often contain articles of interest to the lighting collector.

Collectors' books on glass, ceramics, wood, pewter, tin, iron, silver, etc., usually show many examples of lighting devices.

Among the many books on early living, Gilbert White's *History of Selbourne,* Gertrude Jekyll's *Old West Surrey* and *Old English Household Life* and William Cobbett's *Cottage Economy* describe preparation of rushes while books on *Soap and Candles* by Campbell Morfitt and William Brannt explain the technology and chemistry of candlemaking.

Early encyclopedias such as Rees' *Cyclopedia of Sciences and Literature,* Tomlinson's *Cyclopedia of Useful Arts,* Wylde's *Circle of the Sciences,* and Willich's *Domestic Enclyclopedia* are rewarding as are the many lesser "Domestic Enclyclopedias".

Early catalogs as listed in Lawrence Romaine's *Guide To American Trade Catalogs 1744-1900* are most helpful, and even the recent reprints of early mail order catalogs contain much material on collectible lighting devices and accessories.

EARLY LIGHTING — A Pictorial Guide

CHAPTER I

ANCIENT and PRIMITIVE LAMPS

Following the discovery of fire, primitive man soon learned to conquer darkness. A burning brand snatched from the open fire, plunged into the earth or wedged between rocks, became a torch, giving light, and protection against hostile creatures.

Liquid fuel in the form of animal fat or fish oil burning in a hollow stone or sea shell became possible with the discovery of the principle of the wick, probably at first in the form of dried moss, reeds or grasses. These primitive "lamps" were better suited to relieving the gloom inside the shelter.

As civilization advanced, lamp forms became more sophisticated, although the elements for creating light remained unchanged. The torch of burning wood became a beacon contained in an iron cresset. Lamps of clay and metal, both simple and ornamental, boasted wick channels and spouts, singly and in multiple, and some of the fuel reservoirs now containing vegetable as well as animal oils, were covered. Lamps became slightly elevated, and metal lamps with attached chains could be used as pendant lights.

The cultural development during the classical millenia of lighting history was one of artistic achievement rather than technological progress.

1-1

1-1 SHELL LAMP

The concept of a "lamp" requires a non-flammable fuel reservoir. This need was easily filled for the maritime cultures by the common sea shell.

Description: 5″ l., 3″ w., shell, maritime culture, ca. pre-history.

1-2

1-2 STONE LAMP

Far from the seashore, prehistoric man depended upon the good fortune of finding a naturally hollowed stone, such as this crude specimen.

Description: 4″ l., 2″ w., stone, England (?) ca. 3000 B.C.

1-3 STONE LAMP

As man developed skill with primitive tools, he could improve on nature.

Description: 3″ l., 1¾″ w., 1½″ h., beach stone, Europe (?) ca. unknown.

1-3

1-4 ESKIMO LAMP

The art of ceramics enabled man to duplicate in pottery the crude but useful forms of nature.

Description: 6½″ l., 5½″ w., 2″ h., pottery, Siberia, ca. unknown.

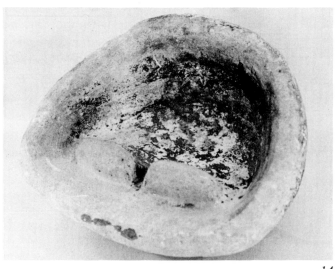

1-4

1-5   ESKIMO LAMP

This small, rounded, oval-shaped lamp is nicely supported by four walrus ivory pegs set in a wooden base.

Description: 4″ l., 2⅝″ w., 1¾″ h.; base 4″ l., 2¼″ w., soapstone, walrus ivory, wood.

1-5

1-6

1-6   ESKIMO LAMP

Large flat lamp, designed to give maximum heat as well as light. The lamp is considered the most important utensil in the Eskimo home. A wick of rolled dried moss or grass laid along the straight edge, burned oil made from seal or whale blubber.

Description: Longest side 18″, decreasing to 9″, 7½″ w., 1½″ d., soapstone, Kodiak Peninsula, Bristol Bay, Alaska.

1-7   HAWAIIAN LAMP

Found in cave in Hawaii in 1875.

Description: 4″ l., 2½″ h., lamp bowl, 3″ dia., stone, Hawaii.

The three primitive stone lamps of North America, (1-5, 1-6, 1-7) are from the newest states of the U.S., Alaska and Hawaii.

1-7

1-8   GRECIAN CLAY LAMP

Shows evolution from the stone lamp, marking the beginning of the ancient classical era in lighting. The lip of the pottery saucer, pinched and turned inward, formed a wick channel; lamp form resembled the scallop shell. Burned olive oil.

Description: 4″ dia., pottery, Cypress, Greece, ca. 600 B.C.

1-8

1-9

1-9   CLASSICAL LAMP

In this lamp, a highly decorated covered oil reservoir is combined with the practical utility of a spout and handle.

Description: 4½″ l., 3″ w., terra cotta, Athenian Agora, ca. 1st century A.D.

1-10

1-10   FIGURAL LAMP

Font fashioned to resemble man's face. Light output was increased through three wicks.

Description: 3″ w., 4″ h., black terra cotta, Alexandria, Egypt, ca. 200 A.D.

1-11   POTTERY LAMP

Pinched open font is mounted on raised stand with integral handle and saucer.

Description: 4″ dia. base, 5″ h., pottery, light green glaze, Morocco, ca. 1400 A.D.

1-11

1-12

1-12   POTTERY LAMP

One continuous rope of clay is fashioned spirally to form reservoir with applied handle and short spout. Brought to America by missionary in 1800.

Description: 3¾″ l., 2″ h., pottery, Palestine, ca. 8th century A.D.

1-14

1-13 PERSIAN SPOUT LAMP

This lamp also utilizes the convenient handle and drip saucer.

Description: 4″ dia., 7″ h., pottery, dark green glaze, Persia, ca. 1400 A.D.

1-14 MULTIPLE WICK LAMP

The principle of multiple wicks — in this case — ten, was an early discovery.

Description: 4½″ l., 2¾″ w., 1″ h., pottery, Mediterranean, ca. B.C.

1-16

1-15 POTTERY LAMP

This single spout lamp incorporates the convenient handle.

Description: 4¾″ l., 3⅝″ h., pottery, blue green glaze, Eastern Mediterranean, ca. 8th Cent. A.D.

1-16 TRIPLE SPOUT LAMP

Nearly 2000 years after (1-14) multiple wick pottery lamps were still being made, (U.S.). Note resemblance in design to (1-15) made over 1000 years earlier.

Description: 9″ l. o.a., 6½″ h., redware, light brown glaze, Pennsylvania, ca. early 19th cent.

1-17

1-17   SPOUT LAMP

The familiar Persian form is here executed in silver on copper with engraved decoration.

Description: 6⅜″ h.o.a., 4½″ dia. base, metal, Persia, ca. 1500 A.D.

1-18   PENDANT LAMP

This lamp incorporated a hinged reservoir cover as well as a chain suspension.

Description: 7¾″ l. o.a., 5½″ h., bronze, Roman Christian.

1-18

1-19

1-19   PENDANT LAMP

As in Fig. 1-18, the symbolic cross and dove appear with the single wick in center of maltese cross design.

Description: 4¼″ l., 3¾″ h. o.a., 1¾″ w., bronze, Roman Christian, ca. 1st or 2nd century, A.D.

1-20   PEDESTAL LAMP

Lamp with 2 wick spouts. Fuel opening in center of sunburst design. Handle in shape of single-winged gryphon, associated in antiquity with fire.

Description: 4″ l., 4½″ h., cast bronze, Roman Empire, ca. 3rd or 4th century.

1-20

1-21

1-21   FIGURAL SPLINT HOLDER

Again, we see the figure of a man's head, in this case used to hold a splint.

Description: 3⅛″ h., 2¾″ w., 2⅞″ d., redware, acquired in Pennsylvania, ca. 1700.

1-22

1-22   PEDESTAL LAMP

This open octagon-shaped reservoir lamp on a pedestal has an iron wick support fastened in the center. Rectangular base has year "1584" cut into one side; letters "IAS" (or "IHS") cut into opposite side.

Description: 7¾″ h.o.a., base 3⅜″ by 3¾″, European.

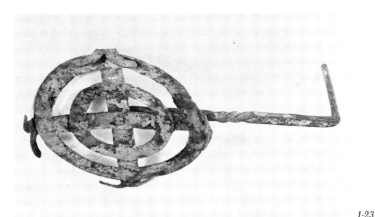

1-23

1-23   BRACKET CRESSET

This shallow cresset is unusual in that it is designed for wall socket mounting.

Description: Cresset pan 9″ dia., 16″ l. o.a., wrought iron.

1-24   SHELL LAMP

The prehistoric scallop shell lamp is still being used in the 20th century, in this case supported gracefully by the spread of prongs of a split stick. The lamp burned fish oil and was in actual use by an AINU family when discovered by the present owner.

Description: 29″ h.o.a., base 11½″ l., 6½″ w., 3¼″ thick, shell and wood, Hokkido Island, Japan.

1-24

1-25

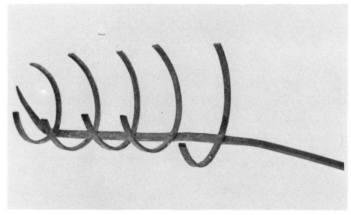

1-27

1-27 CRADLE CRESSET

This "rib cage" type of cresset, burning pine knots, was used largely for night fishing, from the prow of a boat.

Description: Cresset 13″ l., rib span from 3½″ to 6½″, wrought iron, American, ca. 19th century.

1-25 BRACKET CRESSET

This bowl-shaped cresset is designed with a sharp point made to be driven into a wall or timber.

Description: Cresset 6¾″ dia., 13″ h., spike 7″ l., wrought iron, American, ca. 18th or 19th century.

1-26 BASKET CRESSET

The gimbal mounting of this cresset indicates that it may have been used aboard a whaler for burning blubber scraps during the trying-out process at night.

Description: Basket 6½″ dia., 9″ h., wrought iron, American, ca. 18th and 19th centuries.

1-28 ADJUSTABLE FLOOR CRESSET

This tripod base cresset is unusual in that it is adjustable in height from 24″ to 38″.

Description: Cresset 7½″ dia., wrought iron.

1-26

1-28

CHAPTER II
SPLINT and RUSH HOLDERS

Among early lighting devices, the splint and rush holders occupy a position uniquely their own. In design and use, they were of simple folk invention. Both burned solid fuels which were primitive in nature, requiring little skill and virtually no cost in preparation.

Earliest were the splint holders, with wrought iron strips to hold the wood splints, particularly those of resinous pine, called candlewood in early New England, and which burn best in a horizontal position, or at a slightly upward slope. Splint holders with spring clamps or counterweighted jaws were later.

The earliest form of rush holder with its counterweighted jaws may possibly have been a descendant of the heavier splint-holding device, and to some extent, its contemporary in use.

The rushlight, sometimes called the "poor man's candle", is made from the common bog or meadow rush, *juncus effusus,* which grows abundantly in parts of Europe and America.* The rush is cut in late summer and while green is stripped of three-fourths of its cortex, leaving a narrow spine to support the exposed pith. After the peeled rush is thoroughly dry, it is run through melted tallow in an iron boat-shaped vessel called a grisset (13-1, p. 116), and when dry is ready for burning in the holder at a 45-degree angle.

There are many variations of the basic splint and rush holders, some of relative sophistication, examples of blacksmith skill and artistry, as well as those designed to meet special occupational needs.

Accurate attribution of these devices is difficult beyond the fact that splint holders were widely used in Continental Europe, and rush holders commonly used in Great Britain. Long after the splint holder had become a museum relic, the rushlight immortalized by Dickens and Thackeray continued in use well into the late 19th century.

*In Japan, this species of rush is cultivated in the rice fields and the pith used for candle wicks in Japanese candles.

2-1

2-1   SPLINT HOLDER

Although simple and functional in design,
this wedge jaw splint holder mounted in
a crude wooden base, exhibits the
artistic touch of a twisted iron stem.

Description: 6½″ h., wood base 4½″ dia.,
2½″ h., iron and wood.

2-2

2-2   SPLINT HOLDER

With finely wrought spring jaws, this
holder is rare in its heavy forged iron base.

Description: 10½″ h., base 3⅛″ x 2⅞″,
forged iron, Switzerland, ca. 1700.

2-3

2-3   SPLINT HOLDER

The wide twin jaws of this holder would
permit use of two splints at the same time.
The use of stone for a stable base is
extremely rare.

Description: 8¼″ h., jaws ¾″ w., stone
base 3¼″ dia., wrought iron and stone,
Continental Europe, ca. 1600.

2-4

2-4   SPLINT AND CANDLE HOLDER

Although crude in workmanship, this
wedge type holder incorporates an
auxiliary candle socket, a convenience,
although common is rush holders, is
seldom found in splint holders.

Description: 6″ h., oak base 3″ sq., 2¾″ h.,
wrought iron and wood.

2-5   TALL SPLINT HOLDER

Tall tripod based wrought iron holder with serpentine springs, terminating in large flat jaws.

Description: 27½″ h., wrought iron, possibly American.

2-6   TALL SPLINT HOLDER

Heavy wrought iron holder with spring actuated pivoted jaws.

Description: 17¾″ h., 5½″ dia. base, wrought iron.

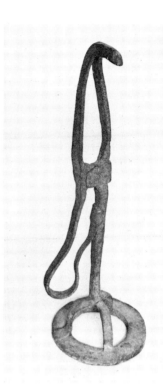

2-5

2-6

2-7

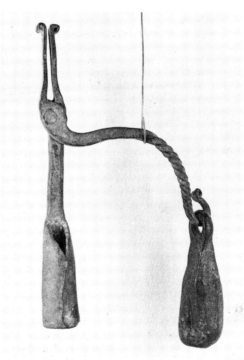

2-8

2-7   ADJUSTABLE SPLINT HOLDER

Tall, adjustable ratchet stand holder on spring clamp-type wooden base. The two jaws permit burning of two splints at the same time but in a horizontal position only.

Description: Wrought iron, ratchet 15½″ l., splint iron rod 18½″ l., wood base 9¼″ l., acquired in Pennsylvania.

2-8   FLOOR TYPE SPLINT HOLDER

Heavy iron splint holder for mounting on wooden floor stand. Pivoted jaws are heavily counterweighted.

Description: Wrought iron holder 9½″ h., iron counterweight 4½″ l.

11

2-9   RUSH HOLDER

The simplest and probably the earliest rush holders borrowed the counterweighted pivoted jaws from the splint holder (2-8, p. 11) and were made for insertion into a wood base.

Description: Wrought iron twisted stem 8½″ h.o.a., wood base 3¾″ h.

2-10   RUSH HOLDER

The blacksmith embellished the iron work with twisted stems and decorated counterweights. Turned wooden base shows further concern with design.

Description: 10″ h., wood base 4⅛″ dia., wrought iron, England, ca. 1750.

2-9

2-10

2-11

2-11   RUSH HOLDERS

In example at right, the wooden base has been superseded by a well designed iron tripod base, adding stability and permanence.

Description: Left: 9″ h., turned wood base 3½″ dia. Right: 7½″ h., iron.

2-12

2-12   RUSH HOLDER

In this example, the smith provided an unusually decorative counterweight, as well as a convenient carrying handle. The nicely fashioned soapstone base makes this a rare specimen.

Description: Iron holder 8⅜″ h., soapstone base 2½″ sq., 1¾″ thick, England.

2-13

2-13   RUSH HOLDER

Small, slender, well proportioned holder
of expert craftsmanship.

Description: 7⅝″ h., wrought iron.

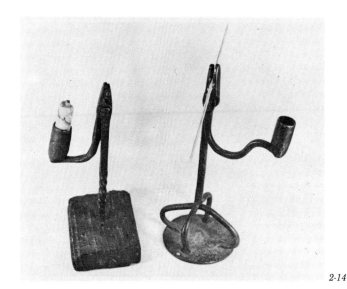

2-14

2-14   COMBINATION RUSH HOLDERS

The use of a candle socket as a counterweight offers a most practical and useful
improvement to the rush holder.

Description: Left: Wrought iron holder
7¼″ h., wood base 3¾″ x 2¾″. Right: 8⅜″ h.,
base 3⅛″ dia., iron.

2-15   COMBINATION RUSH HOLDER

The rush holder, although humble and
utilitarian in purpose, occasionally
provided the blacksmith with an outlet for
artistry, as in this *tour de force* of smithery.

Description: 11½″ h., base 5⅛″ dia.,
wrought iron.

2-16   COMBINATION RUSH HOLDER

The whitesmith has added his fine
finishing touch to this almost formal
polished steel holder.

Description: 10¾″ h., with chamfered steel
jaws, copper washer at base of shaft,
England.

2-15   *2-16*

2-17

2-18

2-17   SPRING RUSH HOLDER

Two interlocking leaf springs provide the gripping power for this beautifully simple rush holder.

Description: 10″ h., wood base 4½″ dia., spring jaws 1⅜″ w., iron.

2-18   SPRING RUSH HOLDER

This unusual spring rush holder has a hook for hanging from a trammel or S-hook.

Description: 9″ h., flat rectangular jaws 3″ w., octagonal wood base, 4½″, iron.

2-20   SPRING RUSH HOLDERS

The tripod base spring type holders are typical of later design. Specimen on right is stamped "M. EVANS" at base of spring jaw.

Description: Left: 10½″ h., Right: 9½″ h., iron, possibly Welsh.

2-20

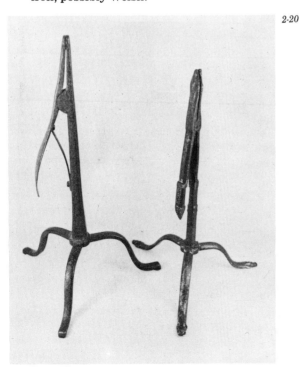

2-19

2-19   SPRING RUSH HOLDER

This rare spring type holder combines polished steel shaft with turned brass base.

Description: 9½″ h., base 3¾″ dia., England, ca. 1800.

14

2-21   2-22

2-21   WOODEN RUSH HOLDER

Wood was rarely used for rush holders due to the need of constant attention to prevent holder from catching fire. Probably home made.

Description: 8¼″ h., wood base, 3″ dia., England.

2-22   SPLINT OR RUSH HOLDER

This ornamented spring type splint holder has jaws that permit its use with rushes.

Description: 25″ h., base 3″ dia., wrought iron, England.

2-23

2-23   ALPINE CANDLE HOLDERS

These Alpine candle holders represent an adaptation of the spring grip principle from the rush and splint holders. They are sometimes confused with rush holders.

Description: Left: 9″ h., base dia., 4″. Right: 10½″ h., base 2¾″ sq., iron and wood, ca. 1750.

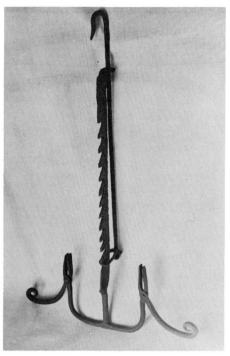

2-24

2-25

2-24   PENDANT RUSH HOLDER

A sawtooth trammel permits the height adjustment of these twin counterweighted rush holders.

Description: 22″ l., as shown, holders 14″ w., wrought iron, Maine.

2-25   PENDANT COMBINATION HOLDER

In this example, to the features of 2-24 has been added the convenience of candle sockets as counterweights.

Description: Trammel 15″ l., sliding rod 17″ l., extends to 32½″ l., holders 10¼″ w., wrought iron.

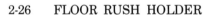

2-26   FLOOR RUSH HOLDER

This combination rush holder with two candle sockets, one a counterweight, is adjustable in height by means of a spring grip on the central shaft.

Description: Adjustable ht., 36″ o.a., cross bar 9½″ w., wrought iron.

2-26

2-27   WALL SPLINT HOLDER

This rare stick-in-the-wall splint holder is pivoted to provide horizontal adjustment.

Description: 18¼″ l., jaws 7″ h., base 4″ w., wrought iron.

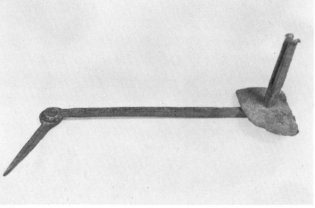

2-27

CHAPTER III

CANDLE HOLDERS

The candle shares with the rushlight the principle of a wick coated with a solid fuel. It differs in its thicker coating, longer life and vertical burning position.

The candle's history is one of both physical and chemical improvements. Wicks evolved from strands of flax, pith of rushes, and twisted fibers which required constant snuffing, to the braided cotton self-snuffing wick of the early nineteenth century, still in use today. At about the same time, the extraction of stearine from fats provided a fuel free from smoking, excessive dripping, unpleasant odors and for the first time a clean bright flame free from care. Many other fuels have been used to a limited extent, including beeswax, bayberry wax, spermaceti and paraffin.

The vertical burning position and the heavier weight of the candle required a special holder. In the same way that candles have evolved, so have their holders. From the early pricket and the simple socket many improvements have been made including drips to catch the wax, push-ups and other devices for removing the stub, adjustable features for controlling the position of the flame, culminating in the spring loaded, self-adjusting candlestick.

The candle holder has been adapted to floor stands, wall sconces and pendant devices including chandeliers. Throughout the centuries it has esthetically reflected the prevailing styles of architecture, furniture and culture. A careful study of the decorative arts of a period is invaluable in the dating and attribution of the candle holder.

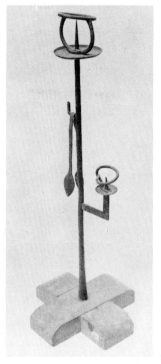

3-1 *3-2*

3-1 PRICKET CANDLE HOLDER

Wooden pricket candlestick, one of a pair. This is the oldest form of a candle holder. The candle was impaled on the sharp spike. Today, its use is limited largely to churches and ecclesiastical ceremonies.

Description: 21″ h., base 6″ dia., wood.

3-2 JAPANESE PRICKET CANDLE HOLDER

This unusual Japanese iron pricket candle holder is of interest because of the auxiliary candle holder and iron snuffing tongs.

Description: 22″ h., wood base 8½″ w., wrought iron, Japan.

3-3

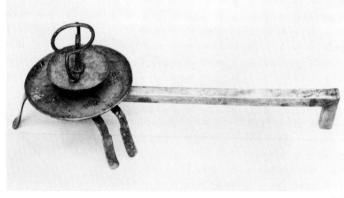

3-4

3-3 TRAVEL FOLDING PRICKET CANDLE HOLDER

This ingenious Japanese traveling candlestick complete with drip, neatly folds into a flat compact package.

Description: Extended 12″ h., folded 3½″ sq., brass, Japan, ca. 19th century.

3-4 ADJUSTABLE PRICKET CANDLE HOLDER

This Japanese pricket candle holder can be adapted for table use as shown, or the adjustable handle can be positioned vertically to raise the candle to a height of from 11½ inches to 18 inches.

Description: Adjustable 11½″ to 18″ l., copper, Kyoto, Japan.

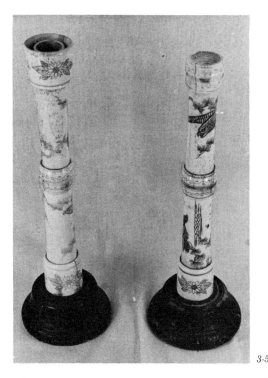

3-5

3-6

3-5   BONE CANDLESTICKS

This unusual pair of decorated whalebone
candle holders are mounted on wooden
bases. Columns are composed of five hand-
cut threaded sections.

Description: 10¾″ h., base 3½″ dia., bone
and wood, ca. 1830.

3-6   DOLPHIN CANDLESTICK

This Dolphin candle holder was made by
the Boston and Sandwich Glass Company.
Its lacy socket makes it the rarest of all
Dolphin patterns.

Description: 9½″ h., base 3½″ sq., glass,
American, ca. 1840.

3-7   BENNINGTON CANDLESTICK

Pottery candle holder with patented
mottled brown "flint enamel" glaze. Made
in Bennington, Vermont by J. & E. Norton
Company.

Description: 8½″ h., base 4″ dia., pottery,
American, ca. 1850.

3-7

3-8   CANTON CANDLESTICKS

Blue and white ceramic candle holders
of a type commonly referred to as
"Canton." These were made in China
for the export market.

Description: 6⅜″ h., base 3¼″ dia., ceramic,
China, ca. 1820.

3-8

19

3-9

3-9   WOOD CANDLESTICKS

Very early pair of heavily carved wooden candle holders with serrated sockets. A matching pair despite slight differences in height.

Description: Left: 9½″ h., base 2¾″ dia., Right: 10″ h., base 2¾″ dia., wood, ca. 17th century.

3-11

3-11   TIN CANDLE HOLDERS

The chamber stick on the left uses a conventional side push up to eject the candle stub. The socket of the holder on the right is cleverly designed with two interlocking projections to act as a "save-all" which permits burning the candle to its very end.

Description: Left: 3¾″ h., base 5½″ dia., tin, brown japanned, Right: 2¼″ h., base 5½″ dia., tin, black japanned, American, ca. 1895.

3-10

3-10   CAST IRON CANDLE HOLDERS

Cast iron provides durability in the small chamber holder on the left, socket screws into the saucer. The Harris Patent candle holder on the right uses a threaded shaft to eject the candle stub.

Description: Left: 3″ h., base 3⅜″ dia., Right: extended 6½″ h., base 3⅜″ dia., imprinted "HARRIS PATENT 1848", cast iron, American, ca. 1850.

3-12   PEWTER CANDLESTICKS

Matching pairs of marked American pewter candle holders are quite rare. These were made by Sellew & Co., Cincinnati, Ohio.

Description: 8″ h., base 4⅜″ dia., imprinted "SELLEW & CO. CINCINNATI", pewter, American, ca. 1835.

3-12

3-13

3-14

3-13 CAPSTAN CANDLE HOLDER

This early type brass holder, also found in bell metal, is provided with a large drip pan and convenient side hole in the socket for candle stub removal.

Description: 5½″ h., base 4″ dia., brass, England, ca. 1650.

3-14 MID-DRIP CANDLE HOLDER

Slightly taller and more graceful than (3-13), holders of this type were imported into the Colonies from England in the latter half of the 17th century.

Description: 8½″ h., base 6¾″ dia., cast brass, English or Dutch, ca. 1660.

3-15 BALL FOOT CANDLE HOLDER

Sophisticated design, superior craftsmanship and the use of bell metal combine to produce an air of elegance in this early specimen. The turned shaft is threaded into the base.

Description: 6⅝″ h., base 4¼″ sq., bell metal, Dutch or English, ca. 1680.

3-16 DOME BASED CANDLE HOLDER

This lathe-turned, heavy cast brass holder has the side hole in the socket for stub removal as in (3-13). Shaft threads into base.

Description: 7½″ h., base 5¾″ dia., cast brass, Spanish, ca. 1680.

3-15

3-16

3-17

3-18

3-17 QUEEN ANNE CANDLESTICK

This diminutive cast brass candle holder is of octagonal design in both base and shaft which precluded lathe polishing.

Description: 6¼″ h., base 3½″, cast brass, English, ca. 1720.

3-18 QUEEN ANNE CANDLESTICK

This cast brass, petal based holder, one of a set of four marked "JOSEPH WOOD", has a shaft consisting of two castings, brazed with vertical seam and expanded into the cast brass base.

Description: 7⅝″ h., base 4″ sq., cast brass, imprinted "JOSEPH WOOD", England, ca. 1760.

3-19 PUSH-UP CANDLESTICK

A rather formal neo-classic design incorporates two highly utilitarian improvements; a practical drip cup, and a central push-up candle stub ejector concealed in the base and connected to a metal disc in the socket by means of an iron wire concealed within the shaft.

Description: 10″ h., base 4¾″ sq., brass, Ireland, ca. 1790.

3-20 BEE HIVE CANDLESTICK

This fairly common design known as "bee hive" type used the central push-up device (3-19). Shaft screws into top of bell shaped base.

Description: 8″ h., base 3″ sq., brass, English, ca. 19th century.

3-19   *3-20*

3-21

3-21   SIDE PUSH-UP CANDLESTICK

A short threaded shaft secures this
elongated socket to an unusually large
base. Decorative pierced handle provides
for side ejection of candle stub.

Description: 7″ h., base 5⅞″ dia., cast
brass, probably English, ca. 1740.

3-23   SIDE PUSH-UP CANDLESTICK

This sophisticated version of the lowly
"hog-scraper" candle holder was
undoubtedly intended for use in the parlor
or bed chamber rather than for kitchen use.

Description: 7¼″ h., base 4½″ dia., brass,
English, ca. 1790.

3-23

3-22

3-22   STUDENT CANDLE LAMP

A fine example of an early double candle
student or desk lamp. Stability is provided
by the weighted tin base which supports
a square iron shaft on which the candle
holders and green painted, pierced tin
shades can be adjusted.

Description: 20½″ h., 15″ w., tin with iron
shaft, purchased in London.

3-24   "HOG-SCRAPER" CANDLESTICKS

Three versions of the familiar "hog-scraper"
candle holder which derives its name
from its similarity to a device (and its
occasional use as such) for scraping bristles
from hogs at butchering time. The small
hook at the top could be used to hang over
the back of a chair or the edge of a shelf.

Description: Left: 8″ h., base 4¼″ dia., spun
brass ring around shaft, Center: 7⅛″ h.,
base 4″ dia., steel ring around shaft,
Right: 6⅝″ h., base 4″ dia., imprinted
"SHAW"; all sheet iron, English, ca. 19th century.

3-24

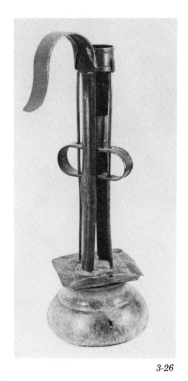

3-25   3-26   3-27

3-25 SPIRAL CANDLESTICK

Carefully twisted strip of iron provides a continuous screw adjustment of the candle for positioning the flame as when used with a water lens (Nos. 11-15, 11-16, p. 105).

Description: 9½″ h., wood base 3⅝″ dia., wrought iron, England, ca. 1750.

3-26 SLIDE CANDLESTICK

In this example, continuous adjustment is obtained by a sliding socket with friction grip. The hooks on many of these sticks provided a means of suspension, as on a loom or chair back.

Description: 8″ h., wood base 3″ dia., iron, European, ca. late 18th century.

3-27 "BIRD CAGE" CANDLESTICK

Adjustable candlestick, similar in principle to (3-26), its name derived from the cage-like appearance of the shaft comprised of six iron wires.

Description: 11″ h., wood base 4¼″ dia., iron, French, ca. 18th century.

3-28 SPIRAL CANDLESTICK

Similar in principle to (3-25). Wrought iron footed pan base adds convenience and stability.

Description: 8″ h., base 5″ dia., wrought iron, European, ca. 18th century.

3-29 ADJUSTABLE CANDLESTICK

Three notches in this sheet iron candlestick provide adjustment to four positions as candle burns. Shaft is supported by rimmed saucer base.

Description: 6″ h., base 4¼″ dia., iron, European.

3-28   3-29

24

3-30 ADJUSTABLE TWIN CANDLESTAND

Small home made pine candle holder with an adjustable cross arm held in position by a wooden pin and supporting two removable wooden candle sockets.

Description: 15″ h., base 4″ sq., cross arm 10″ l., pine, possibly New England, ca. 18th century.

3-31 ADJUSTABLE CANDLESTAND

Heavy burl base offers substantial support to simple wooden screw which permits adjustment of twin candle arm.

Description: 10½″ h., base 7½″ l., 3¼″ w., wood, American.

3-30

3-31

3-32

3-33

3-32 ADJUSTABLE CANDLESTAND

Sand ballasted conical tin base provides stability for this friction grip, adjustable candle tray. The two sockets are provided with generous drips.

Description: 27″ h., base 5½″ dia., tray 6¼″ l., 2¾″ w., iron and tin, New England, ca. 1840.

3-33 ADJUSTABLE CANDLESTAND

Fine lathe work distinguishes this all-wood candlestand. In addition to a well designed base, the central shaft has a convenient hand grip at the bottom and a finial at the top of the screw. Even the drips are lathe turned.

Description: 12″ h., base 5″ dia., candle arm 7″ l., maple, New England, ca. late 18th century.

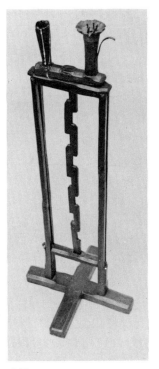

3-34

3-35

**3-34   ADJUSTABLE FLOOR
          CANDLESTAND**

Unusual zigzag ratchet is controlled
by the position of the cross bar at the top
which supports both a sheet iron candle
socket and a "save-all" for burning a
candle stub to the very end.

Description: 29½″ h., extends to 46″ h.,
cross bar 6″ w., pine, probably American,
ca. early 18th century.

**3-35   ADJUSTABLE FLOOR
          CANDLESTAND**

Slightly resembling (3-34), this stand
uses the same sawtooth principle found
in many trammels. Pawl holds the
rachet in desired position. Contoured
base of maple gives stability to oak
frame and ratchet.

Description: 24″ h., extends to 38″ h., base
12¾″ w., cross bar 8½″ w., wood, American.

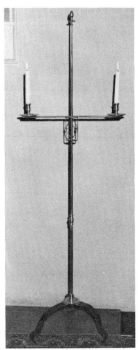

3-36

**3-36   ADJUSTABLE FLOOR
          CANDLESTAND**

Wrought iron adjustable stand with tripod
base. A friction grip supports the cross
arm holding two brass candle sockets. The
round upper shaft topped by brass
finial, permits both rotation and vertical
adjustment.

Description: 63″ h., cross arm 21″ w.,
wrought iron with brass trim, American,
ca. 18th century.

**3-37   ADJUSTABLE FLOOR
          CANDLESTAND**

Adjustable wooden candlestand, Windsor
type. Table height and candle height
both adjustable on main screw. Two screws
in cross bar to remove candle stubs.

Description: 37″ h., main screw 15½″ l.,
table 14½″ dia., legs 16½″ l., wood,
Massachusetts, ca. 1790.

3-37

3-38

3-38   CHANDELIER

Small six-branch chandelier with two tiers of wooden candle sockets mounted on iron wire arms.

Description: Center hub 7″ l., 2½″ dia., arms 9″, wood and iron wire, New Jersey, ca. 1800.

3-40   CHANDELIER

Four-candle chandelier. Turned wooden hub with four heavy wire candle arms, each carrying a wooden candle socket with integral drip. The eye for hanging is blacksmith forged.

Description: Center hub 18″ l., arms 6″, wood and iron wire, Connecticut, ca. 18th century.

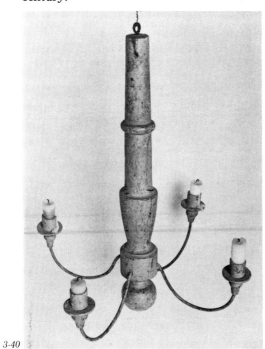

3-40

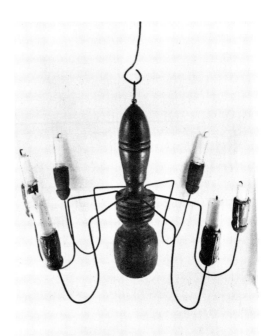

3 39

3-39   CHANDELIER

Six-branch chandelier. Pine candle sockets supported from turned maple hub by iron wire arms. Traces of reddish brown paint on wooden parts.

Description: Center hub 12″ l., 3″ dia., wood and iron wire, New England, ca. 18th century.

3-41   CHANDELIER

Six-branch chandelier, tin and wood. From the first meeting house in Bethel, Connecticut; made by a Bethel tinsmith.

Description: Center hub 19″ l., 4″ dia., arms 10″, fluted holders 3″ dia., wood, tin and iron wire, Bethel, Connecticut, ca. 1800.

3-41

3-42

3-42　REFLECTOR CHANDELIER

Tin chandelier with tin shade and smoke
bell. The four-candle unit is removable
from the shade by unhooking the vertical
rod. Small trays provide drip protection.

Description: 29″ l., shade 5½″ by 12¼″,
candle trays, ea. 5″ l., 2″ w., tin and iron
wire, Redding, Conn., ca. 1800.

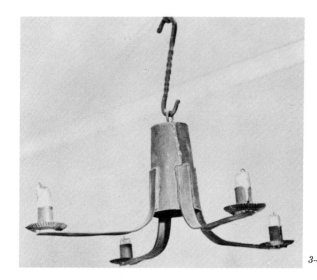

3-43

3-43　CHANDELIER

This simple example of the tinsmith's
art uses four candle sockets with fluted
drips, supported on cylindrical body
by strap tin arms.

Description: 9″ h. (hook not a part of
the lamp), 20″ dia. o.a., tin, American,
ca. 19th century.

3-44　CHANDELIER

This five-branch chandelier shows a high
degree of both design and workmanship.
Note the use of identical pairs of cones
to form the body and finial, and the fluted
saucer to form the canopy at the top.

Description: 22″ l., center cones 6″ dia.,
tin, American, ca. 1820.

3-44

3-45　CHANDELIER

A four-branch tin chandelier of simple
design with strap arms tapering slightly
from cone body to the base of the unusual
deep drip pans.

Description: 31″ l., incl. suspension rod,
center cones 11″ l., 6½″ dia., tin, American,
ca. early 19th century.

3-45

3-46 PENDANT CANDLE HOLDER

Socket can be rotated to position candle. Many of these pendant holders were used in connection with weaving and are often known as loom lights.

Description: 11½″ l., socket arms 3½″ o.a., wrought iron.

3-47 ADJUSTABLE PENDANT CANDLE HOLDER

Familiar sawtooth ratchet permits vertical adjustment while the pivoted suspension provides double duty as a rush holder.

Description: 16″ l., extended 28″ l., wrought iron.

3-47

3-46

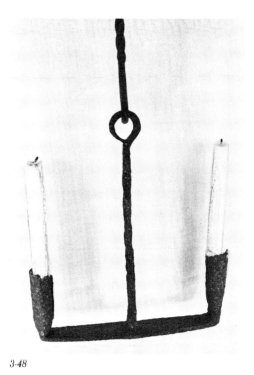

3-48

3-49

3-48 TWIN PENDANT CANDLE HOLDER

Wrought iron sockets formed from the ends of horizontal arm. Twisted iron shaft.

Description: 14½″ l., 7½″ w., wrought iron, ca. 18th century.

3-49 PENDANT CANDLE HOLDER

Simplest form of loom light. These were sometimes hung from a horizontal iron rod fastened to the front of the loom.

Description: 19″ l., socked 2⅝″ l., wrought iron, American.

3-50

3-50   TIN CANDLE SCONCE

In this appealing sconce, the tinsmith
has tooled a design to simulate the more
expensive and more efficient mirrored
sconce (3-52).

Description: 9¾″ dia., tin, American.

3-52   MIRRORED CANDLE SCONCE

Segments of mirrored glass have been
carefully applied to a dished tin support
to provide a parabolic type of reflector,
greatly increasing the effective candle
power. The oval shape is unusual.

Description: 11″ o.a., reflector 9″ h., 6″ w.,
3¾″ d., tin and glass, American.

3-52

3-51

3-51   BRASS CANDLE SCONCE

The polished brass of this richly
ornamental sconce fulfills its function
as a reflector as well as being
decorative. The deep tray offers good
protection against dripping.

Description: 8″ h., 7″ w., brass, Western
Europe, ca. 17th century.

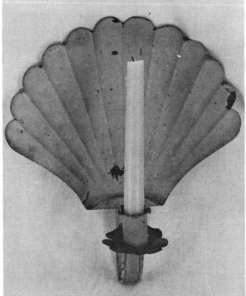

3-53

3-53   PAINTED COPPER CANDLE
SCONCE

The reflectivity of this scalloped, fan-
shaped copper sconce (one of a pair) is
enhanced by the use of light yellow paint.

Description: 12″ h., 10″ w., painted copper,
France, ca. late 18th century.

3-54

3-54   TIN SCONCE

This highly decorated sconce is typical of the tin folk art of New Mexico. Made of thirty-eight pieces of bright tin, with copper disc in the center.

Description: 20″ l., 14″ w., tin and copper, American, ca. 19th century.

3-55   TIN SCONCE

In this narrow tin sconce, the reflector panel has been both decorated and strengthened by beading while the circular top has the conventional crimping.

Description: 13⅝″ l., 2⅞″ w., tin, American.

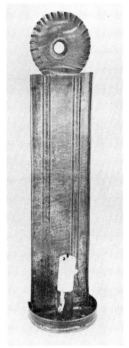

3-55

3-56   TIN SCONCE

Many variations of design appear in these narrow tin rectangular sconces. This example has an unusually deep tray.

Description: 11¾″ l., 3″ w., tin, American, ca. 18th century.

3-57   TIN SCONCE

The semi-circular top of this sconce (one of a pair) further illustrates the many decorative variations contrived by the tinsmith.

Description: 14″ l., 4⅛″ w., tin, American.

3-58   MORAVIAN TILE SCONCE

Although of the early twentieth century, this sconce represents the revival of Moravian ceramic art achieved by Dr. Henry Mercer, Doylestown, Pennsylvania. Patterns were adapted from molds used in the tile works.

Description: 10¼″ l., 4½″ w., green and terra cotta glazed tile, American, ca. 1910.

3-56   3-57   3-58

3-59

3-60

3-59   PIERCED TIN LANTERN

Pierced tin lanterns provided a convenient and safe method of carrying a lighted candle to the barn or on horseback. Half-round lanterns such as this are quite uncommon, as is the chimney arrangement. When out of the wind, the door was opened to emit more light.

Description: 14½″ h., 7½″ w., 4½″d., tin, Massachusetts.

3-60   CANDLE LANTERN

Unusual lantern made from a blown flip glass. The top pierced cone hinges and the pan is lowered into the glass as a separate piece.

Description: 9¾″ h.o.a., base 3½″ dia., glass 5⅝″ h., tin and glass, Massachusetts, ca. 1810.

3-61   PIERCED TIN LANTERN

The flat side of this half-round lantern has the usual glass door which although breakable could emit light in heavy drafts. The fine quality of piercing and the carrying handle at the back made this example noteworthy.

Description: 13″ h.o.a., 7″ w., 4½″ d., tin and glass, Massachusetts.

3-62   PIERCED TIN LANTERN

More typical in design, this lantern has an external candle socket in which the lighted candle could be placed when in locations free from draft. Initials "JF" worked into the design on the door.

Description: 12½″ h.o.a., 6⅜″ dia., tin, Connecticut.

3-61

3-62

3-63

3-64

3-63   WOOD LANTERN

As in this example, these wood lanterns
were usually pinned together with
small wooden pegs. The corner posts
project through the base forming feet. The
dome chimney and bail handle are typical.

Description: 9¾″ h., 7⅛″ sq., wood and
glass, ca. 1700.

3-64   HORN LANTERN

This lantern, originally spelled lanthorne,
derives its name from the use of cow
horn for the windows. A strap tin ring
provides a convenient handle for carrying
or hanging. Three hooded ventilators
furnish the necessary draft.

Description: 17½″ h.o.a., 7″ dia., tin and
horn, English, ca. 1750.

3-65

3-65   WOOD LANTERN

Note the chamfered base and top, and
the chamfer on the corner posts.
The cotter pin hinges lend interest to
this example in pine.

Description: 10″ h., 5½″ sq., pine and
glass, ca. 19th century.

3-66   MICA LANTERN

The design of this lantern resembles
the horn lantern (3-64), but the use of mica
provides a window that is more efficient
and impervious to heat.

Description: 13″ h., 6¼″ dia., tin and mica,
American, ca. 18th century.

3-66

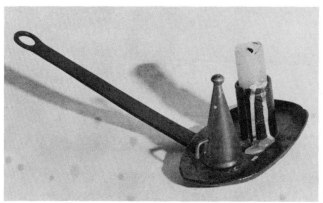

3-68

3-67

3-68   SCOTTISH CANDLE HOLDER

The oval pan of this wrought iron
candle holder has in addition to a candle
socket, an iron cone on which the
extinguisher was kept.

Description: Pan 4¾″ l., 2⅞″ w., handle
6¾″ l., wrought iron, Scotland.

3-67   SPRING CANDLE HOLDER

This patented holder of 1864 is not only
adjustable but incorporates the convenience
of spring loading, a glass chimney to
protect from drafts, an efficient reflector,
and even a built-in extinguisher.

Description: 14″ h., reflector 5″ dia.,
holder marked "DR. HINES PAT. MAY
10, 1864", brass and glass, American,
ca. 1864.

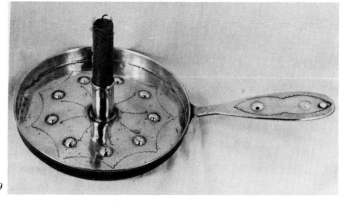

3-69

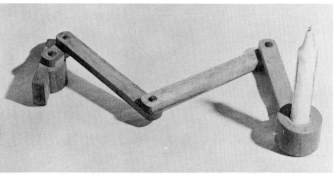

3-70

3-69   FRY PAN CANDLE HOLDER

Fry pan type of candle holder formed
of sheet brass with simple hammered geo-
metric decoration.

Description: 7⅜″ dia., 1″ d., brass, Dutch,
ca. 17th century.

3-70   EXTENSION CANDLE HOLDER

Elbow jointed extension holders of this
type in wood or iron were often mounted
to a work bench. They offer the maximum
flexibility in utilizing the feeble light
of a single candle.

Description: Extends to 20″ l., wood.

34

CHAPTER IV

GREASE and OIL LAMPS

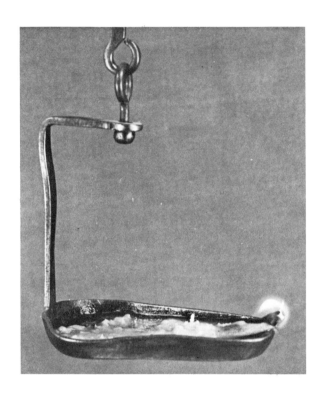 

The supply of oil or grease must be kept available to the wick without overflowing. Heavy oils and grease must be melted before they will respond to the capillary action of a wick while lighter oils tend to overfeed and to drip.

The simple pan lamp required little ingenuity beyond the use of heat conducting materials when grease was to be the fuel. The wick was merely laid against the edge of the pan to expose enough to support the flame. This resulted in a tendency for the fuel to drip.

The drip problem was solved to some extent by various forms of drip catchers or saucers located beneath the lamp, as in the case of the double crusie.

The wick channel accomplished little, but undoubtedly led to the important discovery of the wick support as used in the betty lamp which ensured that any dripping from the wick would flow back into the reservoir.

The use of metal provides sufficient conductivity to keep the heavy oils and lighter greases fluid, while special copper conducting strips were necessary with the heavier greases.

Various canting arrangments ensure a proper supply of fuel to the wick while trunnion or swivel suspensions guard against spillage, and drip pans and saucers make for neatness.

4-1

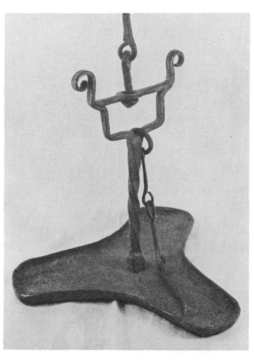

4-2

4-1   JAPANESE TEMPLE LAMP

Wrought iron "snakes" provide support for the two shallow saucers as well as form a hook from which the lamp may be suspended. The diminutive brass lantern merely serves as a weight to submerge and position the rush wick.

Description: saucers 4⅝″ dia., lantern wick holder 1¼″ h., brass and iron, Kyoto, Japan.

4-2   PENDANT GREASE LAMP

This nicely forged three-lobed pan lamp is supported by a swivel suspension. Attached is a small tool for scraping heavy grease to within heating range of the wick, and when necessary, adjusting the wick.

Description: 21″ h., inc. 14″ hook, base 7¾″ w., wrought iron, American, ca. 18th century.

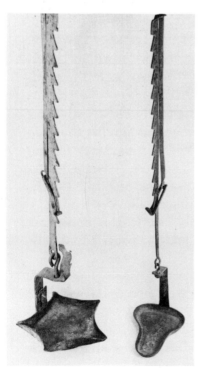

4-3

4-3   ADJUSTABLE PENDANT PAN LAMPS

The familiar sawtooth trammels permit vertical adjustment and swivel supports insure horizontal position of pan. Lamp on left shows the beginning of the wick channel principle.

Description: Left: 4½″ l., 3¼″ w., trammel 21″ l., extended 31″ l., Right: 4¾″ l., 3¾″ w., trammel 24″ l., extended 33″ l., wrought iron, Switzerland, ca. 18th century.

4-4   ADJUSTABLE TABLE PAN LAMP

This tripod base pan lamp with four crude wick channels is adjustable vertically on a central stem by means of a forged spring grip below pan.

Description: 21½″ h., pan 4½″ l., 5″ w., wrought iron, European, ca. 18th century.

4-4

4-5

4-5 CANTING CRUSIE

The crusie is a simple wick channel lamp without internal wick support. In addition to the usual swivel suspension, the bowl of this crusie is provided with a ratchet arrangement to permit a canting action.

Description: 8″ h.o.a., 5¾″ l., 3¾″ w., wrought iron, English, ca. 17th century.

4-7

4-6

4-6 COVERED CRUSIE

This graceful crusie complete with wick pick is unusual in that the bowl is covered.

Description: 7″ l., 5½″ w., wrought iron, ca. 18th century.

4-8

4-8 PENNSYLVANIA FAT LAMP

The bowl of this unusual pottery lamp has a distinct wick channel. The wide saucer base is designed to catch any drip.

Description: 6¼″ h., top 3¾″ dia., base 5½″ dia., stoneware with dark brown glaze, Pennsylvania.

4-7 HINDU LAMP

In this finely decorated, open bowl upright lamp, the wick channel shows the evolution toward the completely enclosed spout.

Description: 7″ h., top 3″ dia., base 3¾″ dia., brass, India.

4-10

4-9

4-9   DOUBLE WICK CRUSIE

As in the case with pan lamps, two or more wicks could be used to provide more light. This is unusual in a crusie.

Description: 3¾″ l., 2½″ w., 2¾″ h., wrought iron, ca. early 18th century.

4-10   DOUBLE WICK GREASE LAMP

This iron lamp cast at Marble Furnace, Adams County, Ohio, is provided with a deep saucer base and integrally cast handle.

Description: 5¼″ h., font 3¼″ dia., base 5½″ dia., cast iron, Ohio, ca. 1830.

4-12   DOUBLE SPOUT LAMP

Although separated by centuries and thousands of miles, this Pennsylvania pottery lamp resembles (4-11) in its saucer, handle and partial spouts.

Description: 5¼″ h., font 3″ dia., base 5″ dia., pottery with black glaze, Pennsylvania, ca. 19th century.

4-11   DOUBLE SPOUT LAMP

This very early terra cotta double wick lamp shows the beginning of the spout principle of the wick support.

Description: 7¾″ h., font 4″ dia., base 4⅞″ dia., pottery, brown glaze, Roman, ca. 7th century.

4-11

4-12

4-13

4-13   TRIPLE WICK BETTY LAMP

In this example, three wicks provide even more light, and here, we see the wick supports, peculiar to the "Betty", which reduced the tendency for the lamp to drip.

Description: 5½" w., 3½" dia., cast brass.

4-14

4-14   MULTIPLE WICK LAMP

Six wick channels are provided in this Near East temple lamp. The generous saucer catches the drip. The eye on the central shaft is provided for suspension.

Description: 7" h., 7" dia., brass, India.

4-16   MULTIPLE CHANNEL LAMP

This four-wick star shaped "crusie" is equipped with a small removable drip pan and swivel suspension.

Description: 5¼" h., with hook 10¾" h., 7" w., small pan 1¾" l., brass.

4-15

4-15   MULTIPLE WICK PENDANT LAMP

This eight-channeled Jewish Sabbath lamp is equipped with a small removable drip pan. The bowl shaped top can act as a funnel for filling the common reservoir through the hollow central column.

Description: 16½" h., cast brass, Russia, ca. 18th century.

4-16

4-17

4-18

4-18   STANDING CRUSIE

The tripod based, scalloped saucer catches the drip in this unusual standing crusie.

Description: 8½″ h., base 4″ dia., sheet iron, Spanish.

4-17   DOUBLE CRUSIE

This is a fine example of the conventional double crusie, also popularly known as a "Phoebe". The serrated stud supporting the upper reservoir permits adjustment as the fuel is consumed; the lower bowl collects the drip.

Description: 11″ h., bowl 6″ l., 3″ w., wrought iron, probably Scotland, ca. 18th century.

4-20   JAPANESE OIL LAMP

The covered reservoir of this pottery lamp with a small wick channel is neatly supported from the wooden upright; a separate saucer collects the drip. When not in use, both pieces are stored in the box that forms the base.

Description: 24½″ h., base 8½″ sq., pottery and wood, Japan.

4-19   WICK CHANNEL LAMP

The lantern shaped support, long narrow wick channel and small drip cup are typical of these early French grease lamps.

Description: 7″ h., 5″ l., brass, French, ca. 1700.

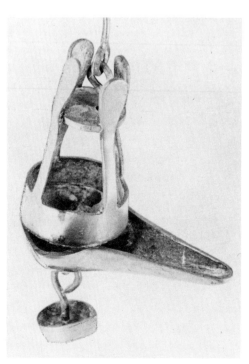

4-19

4-20

4-21 TRUNNION CRUSIE

The trunnion mounting and handle make this a convenient device for portable use.

Description: 7¾″ h., bowl 5″ dia., base 5½″ dia., wrought iron, American.

4-22 KETTLE LAMP

The kettle lamp usually attributed to Pennsylvania is trunnion mounted; the central wick support eliminates the problem of drip.

Description: 8½″ h., font 2″ dia., 1¾″ d., base 5″ dia., wrought iron, American, ca. 19th century.

4-21

4-22

4-23 TRUNNION GREASE LAMP

Unusual pewter trunnion lamp for table or wall mounting. Copper wick tube is used to conduct heat to the heavy fuel.

Description: 7¼″ h., font 3″ dia., base 5½″ dia., pewter and copper, American, ca. 1850.

4-24 COVERED TRUNNION LAMP

This double wick, tripod base lamp is equipped with a hinged "trap door" for filling the reservoir.

Description: 7⅞″ h., iron, Pennsylvania.

4-23

4-24

4-25

4-26

4-25 COVERED BETTY LAMP

The wick support which holds the wick away from the reservoir and prevents dripping, is the significant feature of the popular "betty" lamp.

Description: 4″ h.o.a., 3″ dia., cast brass, American.

4-26 ORNAMENTED BETTY LAMP

Delicate engraving ornaments this all silver Swedish betty. The hinged cover is secured with a small hook and the support is surmounted with a coin bearing the head of Charles XII of Sweden.

Description: 5″ h.o.a., 4″ l., 2¾″ d., silver, coin on handle dated 1713, inscribed "CAROLUS XII, D. G. REX, SVE", Sweden, ca. 1713.

4-27

4-27 P. DERR BETTY LAMP

Among the most sought after betty lamps are those attributed to Peter Derr, the 19th century Pennsylvania gunsmith and lamp maker, often marked "P.D."

Description: 5″ h.o.a., 2¾″ l., 3″ w., l″ d., iron and brass, marked "P. DERR 1840", Pennsylvania, ca. 1840.

4-28 WICK SUPPORT FAT LAMP

The prominent wick support as in this small pottery lamp is quite uncommon among grease lamps of this type.

Description: 2½″ h., top 3″ dia., base 2¾″ dia., pottery, American.

4-28

1 29   4-30

4-29   BETTY LAMP

This clearly shows the important wick support. The typical hook is designed for either suspending from a hook or chain, or fastening into the wall.

Description: 4½″ h.o.a., 4″ l., 3″ w., 1¼″ d., wrought iron, American.

4-30   ADJUSTABLE STANDING BETTY

The familiar spring grip device permits vertical adjustment of this unusual betty lamp. The decorative bird finial is noteworthy.

Description: 21″ h., base 6¼″ dia., lamp 3½″ l., 2¾″ w., wrought iron, English, ca. 17th century.

4-31   IPSWICH BETTY

The combination of a tin betty with a saucered tin "tidy" or stand designed to fit the lamp is attributed to the Ipswich region in Massachusetts.

Description: 11⅜″ h.o.a., lamp 5″ l., 2½″ w., l″ d., stand 7″ dia., tin, America, ca. 19th century.

4-32   PORTSMOUTH BETTY

When the lamp was firmly attached to the base, it is often called a Portsmouth betty. The design is believed to have originated in the Portsmouth, New Hampshire area.

Description: 5¾″ h., 4½″ l., 2⅝″ w., base 6⅝″ dia., tin, American, ca. 19th century.

4-31

4-32

4-33　　　　　　　　　　*4-34*

4-33　FAT LAMP AND TIDY

The central wick support and reservoir of this tin fat lamp resembles the kettle lamp (4-22, p. 41). The wood tidy or stand is assembled from three separate turnings.

Description: Lamp 5″ h., font 1⅞″ dia., stand 6¾″ h., base 4⅛″ dia., tin and wood, Pennsylvania, ca. 1850.

4-34　COVERED KETTLE LAMP

The sliding cover closes the filling hole. The open handle also serves as a hook for a ladder back chair, etc. Tweezers for adjusting the wick are missing from the small bracket on the column.

Description: 8½″ h., font 2¼″ dia., base 3⅜″ dia., tin, Pennsylvania, ca. 1800.

4-35　OPEN STANDING WICK SUPPORT LAMP

The hinged wick support tube permits adjustment of wick angles. The mid-drip also serves to fasten the handle. A lamp of this design is often called a "Convent" lamp.

Description: 10″ h., top 3¼″ dia., base 6″ dia., copper, Dutch, ca. 1800.

4-36　COVERED STANDING WICK SUPPORT LAMP

Fine engraving on cover and base are typical of the ornamentation found on these Dutch lamps.

Description: 9″ h., base 5″ dia., pewter, Holland, ca. 19th century.

4-35　　　　　　　　　　*4-36*

4-37 FLEMISH SPOUT LAMP

A wick channel that completely surrounds the wick becomes a spout. In this lamp, the reservoir and spout snugly fit a cup with a matching channel to catch the drip. The sand weighted bases of these lamps are sometimes flattened at the back to permit hanging as a wall sconce.

Description: 12″ h., font 2″ dia., base 4½″ dia., sheet brass, Flemish, ca. 18th-19th century.

4-37

4-38

4-39 FOUR WICK GREASE LAMP

The square box-shaped central reservoir feeds four rectangular wick spouts made of copper for heat conductivity to permit use with heavy fuels.

Description: 7″ h., font 2⅜″ sq., base 3½″ sq., tin, American, ca. 19th century.

4-38 SPOUT LAMP

Somewhat similar to (4-37), this pewter example with handle is not intended for wall mounting.

Description: 9″ h., base 5″ dia., pewter, Holland, ca. 1850.

4-40 LUCERNA

A fine example of the Mediterranean lucerna with four spouts which burned olive oil. The reflector can be adjusted on the central shaft by means of a thumb screw. Snuffers, tweezers and extinguisher are often attached to these lamps by chains.

Description: 16″ h., base 6″ dia., brass, Spanish, ca. 1700.

4-39

4-40

4-41 PUMP LAMP

In addition to the canting principle, pumps of various sorts have been employed to transfer fuel from a large storage reservoir to a point available to the wick. In this example, the upper tube is compressed into the base by hand and returned by a spring.

Description: 11¼″ h., base 3¾″ dia., pewter, French, ca. 19th century.

4-42 PUMP LAMP

In this example, a small thumb lever operates to raise the oil from the reservoir in the base. Although often missing, pump lamps generally used a simple form of drop burner.

Description: 11¼″ h., base 3⅝″ dia., pewter, French, ca. 19th century.

4-41

4-42

4-43 CANTING LAMP

The canting lamp is designed to adjust the reservoir either manually or automatically as the fuel is consumed so that the wick receives an adequate supply without flooding. In this ingenious design, the font is shaped to act as a compensating counterbalance until the last drop of oil is used.

Description: 7⅜″ h., base 6½″ dia., tin, American, ca. 19th century.

4-44 TRUNNION LAMP

The trunnion lamp should not be confused with a canting lamp since the position of the reservoir has no effect on the level of the fuel.

Description: 11½″ h., base 4¾″ dia., iron, Swiss, ca. 1800.

4-43

4-44

4-45

4-46

4-45 CARDAN LAMP

This primitive example nicely illustrates the adaptation by Cardan (in 1550) of the barometric feed principle commonly used in poultry waterers. This permitted a large reservoir to feed the fuel as needed without recourse to canting or pumping.

Description: 3¼″ h., 4½″ front to back, 2⅝″ w., tin, Pennsylvania, ca. 18th century.

4-46 ARGAND LAMP

The Argand principle employs a tubular wick with access for air to the center as well as the circumference. The extra supply of air provides more efficient combustion. In this painted tole sconce, the Cardan principle is used to feed the fuel.

Description: 10″ h., 4½″ w., tin, painted yellow, brass plate at base of wick tube reads "R. BRIGHT late ARGAND & CO. BRUTON ST".

4-47 RUMFORD LAMP

The inventive genius of Count Rumford combined three improvements to provide the best light of his time; the Cardan principle of fuel supply, the Argand principle of combustion and the rack and pinion method of wick adjustment.

Description: 14″ h., font 4½″ l., 2½″ w., shade 4¾″ dia., base 4⅜″ dia., toleware, English, ca. 1800.

4-48 RUMFORD LAMP

Another fine example of the Rumford lamp, in this case using a diffusing glass shade to reduce glare and soften shadows.

Description: 15″ h., glass globe 6″ dia., tin, painted brown, European, ca. 19th century.

4-47

4-48

4-49

4-49   FLOAT LAMP CHANDELIER

Floating a wick in a transparent reservoir is another simple method of feeding the fuel from a generous supply without flooding. Cork floats support the wick and keep it centered to avoid cracking the glass. The fuel floats on a small quantity of water.

Description: Hub 9″ h., 3″ dia., wood and glass.

4-50

4-50   FLOAT LAMP

This dainty night light with hinged decorated shield has a small tin drawer in the base to hold floats, wicks and accessories.

Description: 8¾″ h., glass panels 4½″ h., 3″ w., tin and glass, European, ca. 19th century.

4-51

4-52

4-51   SPOUT LAMP

This single spout lamp is ornamented with dove finial on cover and crown and cross crest, from which hang tweezers and special wick insertion tool.

Description: 7½″ h., brass.

4-52   TRIPLE BETTY STAND LAMP

The three individual betty lamps on this heavy decorated stand are interconnected to share a common fuel supply. Note that the covers hinge on the side and iron wick supports extend a half inch beyond the pewter to protect it from the heat.

Description: 13″ h., base 6″ dia., each lamp 2½″ l., heavy pewter, dated 1700.

CHAPTER V

WHALE OIL LAMPS

Like a family tree, the evolution of oil lamps follows many paths. The two most important paths of development are the fonts and the burners, and it is the burners that are identified with the type of fuel used.

While the typical whale oil lamp could burn any light fuel, and in Europe often burned vegetable oils, the real age of growth in the first half of the nineteenth century centered around the abundant supply of a superior fuel — whale oil, and especially sperm oil.

With a glass font, it was impractical to use a wick support tube and thus the drop burner was devised. A further improvement — the cork burner provided more positive positioning of the wick.

In 1787, the Miles patent agitable lamp for the first time provided competition to the candle in terms of convenience, cleanliness, safety and low cost. The screw burner of the Miles patent could be applied directly to metal lamps but glass lamps required a threaded metal collar to receive the burner.

Whale oil lamps were usually refilled by removing the burner. The burners can be identified by their metal wick tubes projecting approximately one-quarter inch above the disc with a small slot in the tube, to adjust the wick and the tubes extending below the disc into the font.

5-1

5-2

5-1 FREE BLOWN OIL LAMP

This lamp clearly illustrates the single tube tin drop burner which consists of a small disc attached to the wick tube and merely rests on the opening in the font. Fonts designed for drop burners have no neck.

Description: 7″ h., font 1¾″ dia., base 4½″ dia., glass, Spanish, ca. 1850.

5-2 THREE MOLD NIGHT LAMP

A small wafer of cork firmly sandwiched beneath the tin burner discs gently but firmly grips the short neck of the glass font.

Description: 4¾″ h., base 4″ dia., glass, Boston & Sandwich Glass Co., ca. 1835.

5-3

5-3 BLOWN CHAMBER LAMP

This simple hand lamp is equipped with a two-tube cork burner providing more than double the light of the single tube burner. The two-tube burner is sometimes attributed to Benjamin Franklin.

Description: 2⅜″ h., 2½″ dia., glass, American, ca. 1820.

5-4

5-4 TALL FREE BLOWN LAMP

The tall design, larger font and two-tube burner add to the illumination while the cobalt blue glass stem section adds a decorative touch.

Description: 7½″ h., base 4½″ dia., glass, attributed to Bakewell Glass Co., Pittsburgh region, American, ca. 1830.

5-5

5-5 SMALL CHAMBER LAMPS

These free blown lamps illustrate the way the glassblower could combine colors to provide variety in a single basic design. The short neck for cork burners shows clearly. The colored font especially if of dark glass would make it difficult to detect the oil level.

Description: all 4¼″ h., base 4⅜″ dia., Left: cobalt blue font, Right: cobalt blue base, glass, New England Glass Co., ca. 1830.

5-6

5-6 FREE BLOWN HAND LAMP

An applied handle adds to the convenience in carrying this small chamber lamp with cobalt blue base.

Description: 5″ h., base 3¼″ dia., glass, American, ca. 1850.

5-7

5-7 CUP PLATE HAND LAMP

Inverted cup plates were occasionally used as bases for small lamps with free blown fonts and stems. Often, as in this example, the cup plates for this purpose were made extra thick for added stability.

Description: 7″ h., base 3¼″ dia., Webb and Rose cup plate No. 28, Sandwich Glass Co., American, ca. 1830.

5-8

5-8 WHIMSY SPARKING LAMP

The illustration shows clearly how the mold for a decanter stopper was used to shape the font of this miniature sparking or night lamp.

Description: Left: stopper 3¼″ h., Right: lamp 2″ h., 2⅝″ dia., Sandwich Glass Co., American, ca. 1830.

5-9

5-10

5-9 COLORED HAND LAMP

This is an excellent example of an applied handle. The long straight sided neck indicates the possibility that this lamp was intended for use with a screw top burner, such as is shown in (5-13). The puce colored glass is very uncommon.

Description: 6″ h., base 3″ dia., glass, American, ca. early 19th century.

5-10 TEN-BUTTON TALL LAMP

In this *tour de force,* the glassblower was carried away to the extent of using ten buttons to elevate the font.

Description: 9½″ h., base 3″ dia., glass, American, ca. 19th century.

5-11 PRESSED AND BLOWN TALL LAMP

The design of the font and the wide wafer resembling a drip saucer create the illusion of a peg lamp in a candlestick.

Description: 10¼″ h., base 4″ sq., glass, French, ca. 1840.

5-12 PRESENTATION LAMP

The fine applied rigaree decorations and handle mark this blown lamp as a presentation piece.

Description: 7½″ h., base 4½″ dia., glass, American, ca. early 19th century.

5-11

5-12

5-13 ENGRAVED BLOWN AND
PRESSED LAMP

Three glass working techniques are combined in this dignified lamp, the blown and engraved font on a pressed base. Clearly shown is the brass collar for a screw burner.

Description: 8½" h., base 3" sq., glass, American, ca. 19th century.

5-14 WHALE OIL LAMP
WITH SHADE

Somewhat similar to (5-13) this lamp is equipped with a pewter collar and double wick burner which incorporates a clamp to hold the frosted glass globe.

Description: 8½" h., base 3" sq., chimney 5¼" h., 3½" dia., top 2⅝" dia., glass, American, ca. early 1830's.

5-13   5-14

5-15 HAND LAMP WITH CHIMNEY

This small blown night light lamp with applied handle and pressed base, has a pewter collar and burner arranged to hold the small chimney.

Description: 5⅛" h., base 3¼" dia., glass, American, ca. 19th century.

5-16 MILK GLASS LAMP

A blown font is attached to a square plinth base with a lion's head on each corner and a basket of flowers in each panel. Burner and shade holder arrangement are similar to (5-15).

Description: 11⅜" h.o.a., base 3⅛" sq., milk glass, American, ca. 19th century.

5-15   5-16

53

5-17

5-17   MAKE-DO PRESSED LAMP

When the base of a lamp was broken but the font remained intact, further life could be salvaged by providing a new base; in this case, the font is set in a turned wooden base with plaster of paris.

Description: Left: 8″ h., base 3⅞″ dia., glass, Right: 8½″ h., base 4″ dia., glass, and wood, American, ca. 19th century.

5-18

5-18   MAKE-DO BLOWN LAMP

In this example, the visiting tinsmith fashioned a tin base to the still useful blown glass font.

Description: Left: 5¼″ h., base 3⅞″ dia., tin and glass, Right: 5⅝″ h., base 2″ sq., glass, American, ca. 19th century.

5-19   PEG LAMP

The peg lamp provides a practical means of converting a candlestick into a whale oil lamp. It was possible for the tinsmith to provide a separate filler tube which was a big improvement.

Description: 3¼″ h.o.a., 3″ dia., tin, ca. 19th century.

5-20   PETTICOAT LAMP

The familiar petticoat lamp, often with a filler tube, has a peg concealed in the base which doubles its utility by permitting it to be placed in a candleholder or stand by itself. This picture shows the adjustment slots in the wick tubes.

Description: 3½″ h., 2¼″ dia., tin, japanned, ca. 19th century.

5-19

5-20

5-21

5-22

5-21   TRUNNION HAND LAMP

Handle with thumb grip and trunnion mount combine to make this a handy chamber lamp of cast brass with spun saucer.

Description: 5″ h., base 3¾″ dia., brass, probably English, ca. 19th century.

5-22   MILES TYPE NIGHT LAMP

Two brass spinnings are neatly joined to form a font that, although unsigned, resembles the Miles patent lamp, (9-2, p. 78). The single wick and small font indicate its use as a night lamp.

Description: 6½″ h., base 3½″ dia., brass, ca. 19th century.

5-23   CAST BRASS LAMP

This small cast brass lamp resembles candlesticks both in design and fabrication. Two identical halves were brazed together before turning. Stem is riveted to base.

Description: 7″ h., base 3¼″ dia., cast brass.

5-24   HEAVY CAST BRASS LAMP

The font and stem of this lamp were cast in one piece by using a sand core. The stem screws into the base.

Description: 8¼″ h., base 4¼″ dia., cast brass, wt. 4 lbs.

5-23

5-24

5-25

5-26

5-25   SPARKING LAMPS

Bell shaped sparking lamps with applied handles appear in many sizes in pewter and britannia. The large flat base provides maximum stability.

Description: Left: 1⅜″ h., base 1½″ dia., Right: 2″ h., base 2¾″ dia., pewter, American, ca. 1800.

5-26   COURTING LAMP

This dainty courting lamp equipped with a single screw burner, has a saucer base and ring handle.

Description: 3¼″ h., base 3¼″ dia., pewter, ca. 19th century.

5-27

5-28

5-27   CYLINDRICAL FONT LAMP

Like the glassblower, the pewterer combined various stems with different font forms to achieve variety. This cylindrical form by Trask is an early example.

Description: 6½″ h., base 4″ dia., font 2″ h., pewter, marked "TRASK", American, ca. early 19th century.

5-28   TRUNCATED CONE LAMP

The font of this lamp is known to pewter collectors as "truncated cone". Other form types are lozenge, lemon, acorn and urn. (See p. 63-64).

Description: 7¼″ h., base 4⅞″ dia., pewter, ca. 19th century.

5-29

5-30

5-30   DOUBLE CARDAN LAMP

In this rare example, the large cardan reservoir feeds the fonts of two double whale oil burners.

Description: 8½″ h., base 5″ dia., pewter, American, ca. 19th century.

5-29   CARDAN LAMP

Although not common, the cardan principle was utilized in whale oil lamps. This is a fine example.

Description: 8″ h., base 4¾″ dia., font 3¼″ dia., tin, marked "PATENT APPLIED FOR", New England, ca. 1840.

5-32   CIGAR LIGHTER

A tobacconist's or hotel cigar lighter, this whale oil lamp is surrounded by three miniature "cape cod" lighters consisting of a wick at one end of a short rod and a ball handle at the other. A small fuel supply in each cylinder keeps the wick ready for use.

Description: 4¾″ h., 2½″ dia., silver-plated brass, American, ca. 1840.

5-31

DOUBLE CARDAN LAMP

Here the glassworker has followed the example of the pewterer (5-30) and the tinsmith (5-29) to provide an elegant and useful lamp in the Diamond Thumbprint pattern.

Description: 11½″ h., base 6⅜″ dia., fonts 1¾″ dia., pressed glass, New England, ca. 1850.

5-31

5-32

5-33   RAILROAD LANTERN

The perforated tin base and top collar combine with a blown glass globe with cut design, to provide an ideal lantern for use with a whale oil lamp. The large wire bail is designed to encircle the conductor's arm, leaving both hands free.

Description: 13″ h., 5¾″ dia., tin and glass, New England, ca. 1851.

5-34   ONION LANTERN

The glass font and cork burner in this small hand lantern with spherical globe date it as an early example.

Description: 8¼″ h.o.a., base 2½″ dia., globe 3″ h., 4″ dia., tin and glass, American, ca. 1830.

5-33

5-34

5-35   ONION LANTERN WITH GUARD

A soldered wire guard protects the blown globe. As in (5-34), the base holding the whale oil lamp is detachable by means of a bayonet joint.

Description: 12″ h., base 4½″ dia., globe 7″ dia., tin and glass, New England, ca. 1839.

5-36   AMETHYST ONION LANTERN

The deep amethyst colored globe would indicate this lantern was used for decorative or signaling purposes rather than illumination. The tin whale oil lamp is removed by compressing two latches recessed in the bottom.

Description: 13″ h., base 6¼″ dia., globe 6½″ dia., tin and glass, New England, ca. 1848.

5-35

5-36

5-37 CONFIGURATED GLOBE LANTERN

The configurated glass globe produced primarily for novelty could in some cases add to the strength and achieve slight refractive benefits as in this heavy horizontally ribbed example.

Description: 15″ h.o.a., base 5½″ dia., globe 6½″ dia., tin and glass, New England, ca. 1830.

5-38 CONFIGURATED GLOBE LANTERN

This vertical melon ribbed globe of quarter-inch thick glass improves the strength and beauty but has little refractive value.

Description: 16″ h.o.a., base 4″ dia., globe 7″ dia., wt. 3¼lbs., tin and glass, American, ca. 1830.

5-37

5-38

5-39 CONFIGURATED GLOBE LANTERN

This deeply figured globe was blown in a mold to simulate hobnails and lenses. The refractive value of a blown "lens" is illusory. Although blown in a mold, these thick lenses do exhibit some refraction. This example is unusual in having a glass lamp with a double tube cork burner.

Description: 12¾″ h.o.a., base 3¾″ dia., globe 5″ sq., American, ca. 19th century.

5-40 CONFIGURATED GLOBE LANTERN

The chain ring decoration on this lantern is similar to the decoration on decanters and other glassware made by the New England Glass Company, and contains a glass lamp.

Description: 16″ h.o.a., base 4″ dia., tin and glass, New England Glass Co., ca. 19th century.

5-39

5-40

5-41　DARK LANTERN

This square tin lantern with three glass windows is equipped with sliding shields which protect the glass in transit and can also control the emission of light. The back panel bears a reflector. The square whale oil lamp fastens securely in place.

Description: 9″ h., base 3¼″ x 3¾″, tin and glass, ca. 1830.

5-42　WALL LANTERN

This handsome wall lantern has a polished brass reflector and is equipped with both a candle socket and a peg adapter for the oval whale oil lamp with a drop burner. Front door hinges for access.

Description: 11⅜″ h.o.a., base 7″ w., 3¾″d., reflector 3½″ dia., tin, brass, glass, ca. 1800.

5-41

5-42

5-43

5-43　MORLEY LANTERN

This patented lantern consists of a glass font and globe blown in one piece with a glass separator designed to hold the double tube whale oil burner. Access to burner and font is through the hinged top. While patented by Philemon Morely, Brooklyn, N. Y., October 7, 1854, this lantern marked "Patent Applied For" precedes the patent date.

Description: 10½″ h., base 4½″ dia., wire guard 7″ dia., tin, glass, marked "PATENT APPLIED FOR", American, ca. 1854.

5-44　DARK LANTERN

Two hinged doors protect the mica window, and a strap handle on rear permits its use as a dark lantern. The beehive font of the single tube lamp, soldered to the bayonet attached base plate is clearly shown.

Description: 9″ h., 2⅞″ dia., base 3½″ dia., mica, tin, painted green and yellow.

5-44

CHAPTER VI

BURNING FLUID LAMPS

Near the middle of the 19th century, efforts to further improve the efficiency of lamps resulted in dozens of mixtures, many patented, known as burning fluids. Nearly all consisted of turpentine (camphine) and alcohol in various proportions and some included naptha or benzine. They all were highly volatile and of low viscosity and low flash points, all of which made them hazardous if not carefully handled. Many explosions occurred due to careless filling or the breakage of glass lamps.

New burners were designed which were interchangeable with the whale oil burners to permit conversion to the new fuel and simplify manufacture. Except for the few patented safety features, there was no special change in the lamps themselves. The burners which came with one to six brass tubes, usually tapered, are longer than whale oil tubes and in the case of multiple burners are splayed. The tubes did not project down into the font thus keeping heat away from the volatile fuel. Although often missing, small metal caps attached by chains were furnished to extinguish the flame but primarily to retard evaporation of the volatile fuel.

6-1

6-1 SPARKING LAMPS

These diminutive lamps show clearly the tapered camphine burners and captive wick caps.

Description: Left: 4¼″ h., 12-sided font 2″ dia., base 1¾″ dia., Right: 4¼″ h., 2-part mold font 2⅛″ dia., base 2″ dia., glass, brass, American, ca. 19th century.

6-2

6-2 SPARKING LAMP

This small blown in a mold lamp in the cable pattern commemorated the laying of the first Atlantic cable in the 1860's. Single tube burners are sometimes straight while multiple burners are usually tapered.

Description: 4½″ h., base 2″ dia., pattern glass, American, ca. 19th century.

6-3 BLOWN AND PRESSED LAMP

The important feature of this lamp is the pressed base which matches the first pressed glass tumbler made at Sandwich in 1827. This would indicate that the lamp was originally made for whale oil.

Description: 13½″ h., base 4½″ dia., 3¾″ h., glass, Sandwich, ca. early 19th century.

6-4 BLOWN AND PRESSED LAMP

A heavy molded, three-lobed base is combined with a vertical melon ribbed blown font.

Description: 9¼″ h.o.a., triangular base 4½″, glass, Boston area, ca. 1850

6-3

6-4

6-5   3-WICK BURNER

This unmarked American pewter lamp with an urn-shaped font is equipped with a three-tube burner to produce more light.

Description: 7¾″ h., base 4¾″ dia., pewter, American, ca. 19th century.

6-6   4-WICK BURNER

The pewter collector will recognize the font of this Gleason lamp as the lemon pattern.

Description: 4¾″ h., base 3¾″ dia., pewter, marked "GLEASON", American, ca. 19th century.

6-5

6-6

6-7

6-8

6-7   6-TUBE SCONCE

The six-tube burner and generous font would make this bracket lamp suitable for use in a theater, railroad depot or other public place.

Description: 9¼″ h.o.a., font 3¾″ dia., 2″ h., reflector 6″ h., 4″ w., tin, marked "DIETZ BROTHER & CO NEW YORK", ca. 19th century.

6-8   PATTERN GLASS LAMP

The Boston and Sandwich Company in the 1840's offered a spillholder to match a few of the pattern lamps; this pattern was one of them. While three-tube burners are in a line, four tubes and six tubes are usually arranged in a circle.

Description: 9¼″ h., font 3″ dia., 4¾″ h., base 3½″ dia., glass, Sandwich, ca. 1840.

6-9

6-10

6-9   HAND LAMP

An unusually large marked American example of the familiar bell shape.

Description: 5¾″ h.o.a., base 4¼″ dia., pewter, marked "MOREY & OBER" Boston, ca. 1852.

6-10   CHAMBER LAMP

A lozenge-shaped font mounted on a saucer base with ring handle in this marked American hand lamp.

Description: 4½″ h., base 5½″ dia., pewter, marked "GLEASON", American, ca. 19th century.

6-11

6-12

6-11   PETTICOAT LAMP

The familiar cylindrical font equipped with a handle is mounted on a "petticoat" skirt which conceals the peg as found in tin petticoat lamps. (5-20, p. 54).

Description: 6″ h., font 2¼″ dia., 2″ h., base 3¼″ dia., pewter, American, ca. 1850.

6-12   CHAMBER LAMP

A stem, saucer and ring handle provide yet another variation to the cylinder form.

Description: 6¾″ h., pewter, American, ca. 19th century.

6-13

6-14

6-14 PAIR OF URN LAMPS

This matching pair of urn-shaped font lamps are attributed to William Calder of Providence, Rhode Island.

Description: 8¾″ h., base 5½″ dia., pewter, American, ca. 1850.

6-13 ACORN LAMP

The font of this lamp really combines the acorn and cylinder forms to create an unusual font.

Description: 9″ h., pewter, American, ca. 19th century.

6-15 FANCY LAMP

A gold decorated pear-shaped milk glass font is gracefully supported by an engraved silver base.

Description: 7″ h., base 3½″ dia., milk glass and silver, Sandwich, ca. 1850.

6-16 OVERLAY PEG LAMP

Cranberry and milk glass are combined in the overlay of this handsome peg lamp.

Description: 4″ h., 2″ dia., candlestick 5¾″ h., base 3″ dia., glass, brass, probably Sandwich, ca. 1875.

6-15   6-16

6-17

6-18

6-17   PEG LAMP

A good example of a simple form of a blown peg lamp.

Description: 5″ h., 5″ dia., glass, American, ca. 19th century.

6-18   PANELLED PEG LAMP

Peg lamps were usually used in candle-holders of various types but lent themselves readily to home made holders such as this wooden sconce.

Description: 4½″ h., 2″ dia., glass and wood, ca. 19th century.

6-19   PEG LAMP IN SCONCE

Although this sconce with its drip pan would be practical for use with candles, the tin retaining ring nicely fitting the pear shaped peg lamp indicates that these pieces were made for each other. A device eminently suited for the country tavern on the Delaware River at Hancock, New York, from which it came.

Description: peg 3½″ dia., sconce 10″ h., 6½″ w., glass and tin, American.

6-20   WHIMSY LAMP

The six petal blown font is mounted upside down on a hexagonal pressed base. Neither font nor base are rare but the inverted mounting is unique.

Description: 10″ h., 3½″ dia., glass, American, ca. 1855.

6-19

6-20

CHAPTER VII

LARD and LARD OIL LAMPS

During the two decades of the mid-nineteenth century in America, a third fuel occupied a competitive position with whale oil and burning fluids.

Lard and its by-product, lard oil, were inexpensive and gave a good light, but introduced a new challenge which was to ensure proper combustion. The heavier lard is solid at room temperature and requires a massive transfer of heat to liquify it for the capillary attraction of the wick. Many of the patented lamps further depended upon pumps or canting mechanisms to bring the lard within range of the heat conducting burner parts.

Lard oil extracted from the lard resembled whale oil, and in a warm temperature would burn satisfactorily in almost any whale oil burner. The viscosity of the lard oil, however, increases rapidly with cooler temperatures. Therefore, improved heat conductors were incorporated in lamp burners intended for use with lard oil.

As a general rule, lard oil burners are designed for the production and transmission of heat to the fuel. The burners can be recognized by the wick tube, usually copper, extending a short distance above the font and projecting well down into the oil to act as a heat conductor. Frequently additional heat conducting devices are provided. The wicks are wide and flat or of the annular argand type.

7-1 SOUTHWORTH PETTICOAT LAMP

This petticoat hand lamp is equipped with the Southworth patent burner which features two large wicks to generate heat, combined with copper conducting strip to carry the heat to the lard.

Description: 5¾″ h., base 3″ dia., font 2¼″ h., 2″ dia., burner marked "SOUTHWORTH PAT. JULY 1842", tin, American, ca. 19th century.

7-2 ARGAND LARD LAMP

Here the argand principle is used to provide air through a rectangular tube between the two flat wicks. The air is admitted through the expanded louver arrangement at the base of the stem. The wick tubes are not copper but extend to the bottom of the font. The small tube on the side of the font held a wick pick, missing in this example.

Description: 7½″ h., base 6¼″ dia., font 2¼″ h., tin, probably Pennsylvania, ca. 1840.

7-1

7-2

7-3

7-3 ARGAND LARD OIL LAMP

This argand lamp with annular wick in a copper burner was intended for use with lard oil which could be supplied through the filler tube without removing the burner. Air is admitted through three small holes in the stem just below the font. The reflector serves to redirect the light down on the work.
Description: 9½″ h., base 6″ dia., font 3″ h., reflector shade 6½″ dia., tin, japanned, American, ca. 1850.

7-4 PAINTED LARD OIL LAMP

The cast iron base adds stability as well as artistry to this painted tin hand lamp. The conical shade is designed to spread the light. Reflectors undoubtedly helped to heat the font by reflecting radiant heat from the flame.

Description: 11½″ h., base 5½″ dia., shade 5¾″ dia., tin and cast iron, painted, American, ca. 1830.

7-4

7-5　　　　　*7-6*

7-5　SOUTHWORTH PATENT

The clear glass font permits an unobstructed view of the salient points of the Southworth patent burner: the short converging wick tubes above the burner and the long conducting wick carriers extending far into the font.

Description: 7″ h., base 2½″ sq., glass, American, ca. 19th century.

7-6　SOUTHWORTH PATENT

Note the Southworth burner in an engraved glass lamp font. The deep font does not make for efficient use with lard.

Description: 9″ h., base 3¼″ sq., glass, American, ca. 19th century.

7-7　SOUTHWORTH CHAMBER LAMP

The familiar forms of glass and pewter lamps required only the Southworth burner to become a lard lamp. Judging from the relative frequency of examples found today, the Southworth burner would seem to have been one of the more successful lard burners.

Description: 6″ h., font 2¾″ h., base 5¼″ dia., marked "R. GLEASON", font marked "SOUTHWORTH PAT JULY 1842", pewter, American, ca. 19th century.

7-8　RIBBON BURNER

The low cost of lard as a fuel coupled with a need for heat to liquify it made a wide flat burner a simple practical solution, especially if made of copper. This example shows clearly the three adjustment slots for application of a wick pick.

Description: 7¾″ h.o.a., base 5″ dia., pewter, American, ca. 1850.

7-7

7-8

7-9

7-9   UFFORD LAMP

This is typical of the Kinnear patent as manufactured by S. N. & H. C. Ufford of Boston, showing the three usual features: a filling tube on the left, a wide flat wick in the center, and a small round wick for a pilot or night light on the right. Unusual, however, are the length of the stem and the presence of the reflector shade which is usually missing.

Description: 11″ h., base 5½″ dia., shade 6½″ dia., gilded tin font, stamped on one side "KINNEAR PATENT FEB 4TH 1851", other side "S.N. & H.C. UFFORD-117 COURT ST. BOSTON", japanned tin shade, gilded cast iron base, American, ca. 19th century.

7-10

7-11

7-10   CHAMBERLAIN PATENT

The adjustable drum shaped font carries two flat wicks and a separate filler hole. Spring loaded drum can be rotated to bring fuel to the wick. Sand weighted base lends stability as a table lamp. The reflector support strap is sometimes pierced at the top to permit use as a wall lamp.

Description: 9½″ h., base 3⅛″ sq., tin, American, ca. 1854.

7-11   CANTING LAMP

A different shaped font and positioning arrangement may have been an attempt to circumvent the Chamberlain patent (7-10). The deep rectangular footed tray base catches the drip.

Description: 6½″ h., base 4¼″ x 4¾″, tin, American, ca. 19th century.

7-12   CARDAN LARD OIL LAMP

Since the large cardan reservoir could only be filled through the lamp font and was insulated from heat by the reflector, this lamp must have used lard oil or other liquid fuel.

Description: 10¼″ h., base 3⅝″ l., reflector 5″ h., 3½″ w., tin, ca. 19th century.

7-12

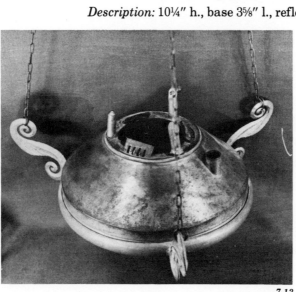

7-13

7-13   LAWRENCE PATENT CHANDELIER

This three-burner version of the Lawrence Patent Chandelier with side filler tube, lacks the chimney. These chandeliers also came with four burners.

Description: 8″ dia., 3″ h., top 4″ dia., pewter, American, ca. 1831.

CHAPTER VIII

KEROSENE LAMPS

The year 1860 marked the beginning of the kerosene era when large quantities of this improved fuel became available with the discovery of petroleum deposits. It remained only to remove the heavy tars and volatile components to produce an illuminant that was clean, efficient and inexpensive.

The forty years of kerosene coincided with the age of invention which yielded a proliferation of patented lamps, burners, chimneys and accessories, and the industrial revolution which made all of these available to the mushrooming population.

The collecting and study of kerosene lighting has only recently begun, now that the period has met the one hundred year definition of "antique", and there is a growing interest in the great variety and ingenuity of the kerosene lighting devices.

8-1   *8-2*

8-1   HAND LAMP

The squat ribbed blown in a three-part mold font has an applied handle for use as a chamber lamp.

Description: 3″ h., 3½″ dia., chimney 6⅜″ h., glass, American, ca. 19th century.

8-2   HAND LAMP

This lamp is similar to (8-1) except for shape of font and the shield pattern. The burners and bead top chimneys on these two lamps are quite typical.

Description: 2½″ h., 4″ dia., chimney 8″ h., glass, brass burner marked "P & A MFG. CO., WATERBURY, CONN-MADE IN USA", American, ca. 19th century.

8-3   MINIATURE LAMPS

The small fonts, burners and chimneys of these miniature lamps were adequate for the small flame required as a night light.

Description: Left: 2″ h., 3″ dia., glass with font imprinted "LITTLE BUTTERCUP", brass burner "Acorn", manufactured by Plume & Atwood, Waterbury, Conn., Center: 2½″ h., 2½″ dia., glass font imprinted "THE HANDY NIGHT LAMP", tin burner, Right: 2″ h., 3″ dia., glass font imprinted "NUTMEG", brass wire handle, all American, ca. 19th century.

8-4   MINIATURE LAMPS

The glass font of the "Little Duchess" lamp on the right is attached to the brass saucer base by the retaining circular spring; on other lamps of this type the bayonet principle is used. The diminutive lamp on the left is a patented night lamp with a milk glass chimney.

Description: Left: 1½″ h., 1¾″ dia., glass font embossed "LITTLE HARRY'S NIGHT LAMP", "L.H.OLMSTED-NEW YORK-PATENTED MARCH 20, 1877", Right: 2″ h., 2¼″ dia., glass font embossed "LITTLE DUCHESS", brass "Nutmeg" burner, American, ca. late 19th-early 20th century.

8-3

8-4

8-5 TABLE LAMP

This pattern glass lamp with its flared hexagonal base has a distinctive elegance. The bulbous chimney adds grace to the appearance of the lamp and is less susceptible to breakage from thermal strains.

Description: Base 9¼″ h., 6″ dia., 16″ h.o.a., pressed glass "drape" pattern, American, ca. 20th century.

8-6 MINIATURE LAMP

This small Bristol glass lamp is equipped with a bulbous chimney which combines a frosted reflector-diffuser mid-section with clear glass top and bottom.

Description: 4⅜″ h., base 3″ dia., spherical font 3½″ dia., beaded globe 4⅜″ h., 3″ dia., glass, Bristol, pink and white floral decoration on font and globe, burner marked "CROWN A.D. & CO.", American, ca. 1895.

8-5   8-6

8-7 TABLE LAMP

In this example of late nineteenth century decorative table lamps, a generous frosted, engraved font is supported by a gilded cast figure of Mary and Her Little Lamb. The heavy cast iron base adds stability to the lamp.

Description: 14½″ h., font 5″ dia., base 5″ sq., figured stem 7½″ h., glass, brass, cast iron, American, ca. late 19th century.

8-7

8-9 RIPLEY "WEDDING" LAMP

A molded glass pedestal is attached by a brass collar to a pressed glass body which supports two mold blown fonts and a central match holder. These lamps appear in various combinations of clear, opalescent, and colored glass. The match holder cover shown in this example is usually missing.

Description: 19½″ h.o.a., base 5¼″ dia., stamped "RIPLEY & CO. PATD. FEB. 1, 1870", fonts each 3¾″ h., 3½″ dia., match holder 3½″ h., 2″ dia., marked "PATENT SEPT. 30, 1870", American, ca. 19th century.

8-8 PARLOR LAMP

The ornamented spherical globe is independent of the chimney and functions solely as a diffuser to soften shadows and glare. The drawbar method of wick control is clearly shown. Although unbreakable, metal fonts lacked the convenience of a visible fuel supply. The cast iron base lends stability.

Description: 21″ h.o.a., bronze font container with silver handles 7″ dia., marked "B & H-Feb. 11, 1890, Feb. 27, 1888, Aug. 20, 1889", American, ca. late 19th century.

8-8   8-9

8-10

8-11

8-10 STUDY LAMP

At the end of the nineteenth century, nickel-plated brass became very popular for utilitarian table and study lamps. A large opal reflecting shade reduced glare and distributed the light over a wide area. Stability is provided by a cast iron ring fixed in the base.

Description: 21″ h., font 6″ dia., stamped "B & H", shade 10″ dia., brass burner stamped "July 1, 1890, Jan. 2, 1898, Aug. 30, 1892, Apr. 23, 1895, Dec. 31, 1895", flame spreader marked "B & H", brass nickel plated, iron, glass, American, ca. 19th century.

8-11 STUDENT LAMP

The horizontal cylindrical font of this patented lamp can be adjusted vertically on the stem which is supported by a weighted base. In a more usual type, a vertical font acting on the cardan principle also serves as a counterweight.

Description: 13″ h., extended 17″ h., font 7″ l., 2½″ dia., W. O. Lincoln patent, Oct. 28, 1879, brass burner marked "LEADER-BRIDGEPORT BRASS CO.", nickel plated brass, iron, glass, American, ca. 19th century.

8-12 PENDANT DOUBLE ANGLE LAMP

A large central reservoir feeds two (and in some examples three and four) angle burners by the cardan principle. The angle burner took advantage of the combination reflecting chimney and clear glass bowl to avoid the usual shadow of the font, making an ideal hanging lamp for stores, offices and public areas. Single and double burner models were also made for wall mounting.

Description: 14″ h., 31″ w.o.a., nickel plated reservoir 9″ h., 5″ dia., 3-qt. capacity, marked on rim of chimney and burner turn-up "ANGLE LAMP CO.-N.Y.", nickel plated, glass, American, ca. 1890.

8-13 PENDANT LIBRARY LAMP

The large dense reflector, although highly decorated provided a wide distribution of diffused light from these hanging lamps. A spring in the canopy counterbalances the chain suspension so that the lamp can be lowered for lighting or filling, and adjusted to any convenient height by the finger ring at the bottom. A small smoke bell is attached to the canopy.

Description: 30″ l. from ceiling to bottom of lamp, extended 60″ l., hobnail glass font with white opaque hand painted 14″ dia. shade, 36 cut glass prisims attached to pierced brass ring, American, ca. late 19th century.

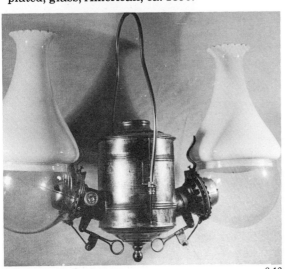

8-12

8-13

8-14   *8-15*

8-15   PAPIER MACHE LAMP

The Fibre Ware Company of Portland, Maine used the Stevens patent principle of (8-14), substituting papier mache for wood on the base and font. The stem is turned from solid wood.

Description: 8½″ h., base and font 5″ dia., papier mache, wood and tin, American, ca. 1875.

8-14   STEVENS WOODEN LAMP

A two-piece tin font is enclosed in a thin wooden shell consisting of two turnings cemented together. The turned maple shaft is threaded on each end for fastening to the font and base. The wood turning was done in Lebanon, New Hampshire with the assembly in Westbrook, Maine.

Description: 8½″ h., base 4½″ sq., wood and tin, G. M. Stevens Patent, Dec. 28, 1875, American, ca. 1875.

8-17   PYRAMID LANTERN

Kerosene was ideally suited for all sorts of lanterns and kerosene burners may have replaced whale oil or lard oil burners in many cases. The hinged rectangular reservoir has a patented burner soldered permanently in place. The wick adjustment wheel extends outside the lantern for easy adjustment or opening. The font is provided with a separate filler hole with a small screw cap.

Description: 8¾″ h., base font 4″ w., 2⅜″ d., burner stamped "ARCHER & PANCOAST", tin and glass, American, ca. 19th century.

8-16   WALL LAMP

The removable glass font is supported by japanned tin ring. The strap tin handle which supports removable reflector has keyhole shaped opening for hanging on the wall. Instead of the usual cemented burner collar, a thin threaded ring is recessed in a molded glass neck and locked with small indentations.

Description: Font 4″ h., 4¼″ dia., bracket 7″ h., reflector 6½″ dia., glass and tin, burner marked "P & A MFG CO. WATERBURY, CONN. MADE IN USA", American, ca. 20th century.

8-16   *8-17*

8-18   TAPLIN BURNER

The Taplin patent covers a simple method of supporting the chimney by means of "spring arms pivotally supported . . . with a number of chimney bearing surfaces" which support the chimney from the inside when the latter is fully inserted.

Description: Turn-up stamped "C.A. TAPLAN CO. PAT 8-23-96", brass.

8-18

8-19   PHOENIX BURNER

This burner combines two ingenious improvements. Clearly shown is the britannia filler tube with captive cover permitting filling while lighted; not visible, a small wire arm raises an extinguisher tube inside the deflector.

Description: Burner manufactured by Phoenix Mfg. Co., Newark, N.J., Patented Oct. 18, 1887, brass and britannia.

8-19

8-20

8-20   RECTANGULAR BURNER

Rectangular and oval burners and chimneys were designed to match the thermal pattern produced by flat wicks in an effort to get maximum draft with minimum chimney breakage. In this example, the slot in the deflector is further contoured to produce efficient combustion.

Description: Manufactured by Bridgeport Brass Co., Bridgeport, Conn., stamped on base "PAT'D Sept. 18, 77, Nov. 18, 79, Apr. 6, 80", brass.

8-21   RADIANT CONE BURNER

The use of transparent glass in place of brass for a deflector cone was intended to increase the light output by transmitting a high percentage of light normally trapped by opaque deflectors.

Description: Manufactured by R. H. Maple Co., Dayton, Ohio and Indianapolis, Ind., Pat. Dec. 18, 1906, brass and glass.

8-22   ELECTRIC ADAPTER

In the same way that kerosene burners were able to supersede whale oil and burning fluid burners, so electric adapters were made to fit on kerosene lamps to take advantage of lighting progress. Most adapters were designed to fit the burner collars. This example takes the place of the glass chimney.

Description: Made by Hubbell Co., Pat'd. Feb. 18, 1902, brass.

8-21

8-22

CHAPTER IX

PATENT

LAMPS

Patent lamps offer both a challenge and a satisfaction to the lighting collector. The challenge is in the search for examples recorded in patent records, some of which were apparently never manufactured beyond the patent model. The satisfaction comes from the ability to identify and document the device and its inventor.

With the exception of the Argand patent of 1784 and the Miles patent of 1787, most collectible patented lamps were patented in the United States. In the seventy years between 1790, when Joseph Sampson was granted a patent for manufacturing candles, and 1860, there were five hundred and fifty-six patents issued pertaining to lighting devices. In the inventive decade that followed, approximately two thousand lighting related patents were granted.

Fortunately, most patented devices bear one or more patent dates (always on a Tuesday) which greatly simplifies research.

Starting in 1826, the Journal of the Franklin Institute lists patents issued each month, and from 1848 through 1871, the annual Patent Office Reports contain a fairly complete description of each patent issued, after which the Patent Office Gazette continues to furnish the same information.

With the name, date and patent number, copies of the original patent papers may be obtained, at nominal cost, from the Office of the Commissioner of Patents, Washington, D.C.

9-1   MILES PATENT LAMP

In 1787, John Miles of Birmingham, England was granted a patent for an "agitable lamp" consisting of a totally enclosed font with a central wick supported by a tube and flange burner which would not readily spill the fuel when agitated.

Description: 5½″ h., brass with embossed plate "MILES PATENT", ca. late 18th-early 19th century.

9-2   MILES PATENT LAMP

A tall lamp also bearing the Miles label. Although most whale oil lamps used the Miles principle, marked lamps are extremely rare.

Description: 10½″ h., brass with pewter marked "MILES PATent", ca. late 18th-early 19th century.

9-1

9-2

9-3   SEWELL PATENT

On October 2, 1847, Thomas Sewell of New York was granted a patent No. 5,311 for "an improvement in lard lamps". When the base of the lamp is turned, the lard is forced up to the wick tubes where conducted heat can liquify it.

Description: 7½″ h., base 6″ dia., tin, japanned, American, ca. 19th century.

9-4   MALTBY NEAL PATENT

On May 4, 1842, patent No. 2,604 was issued to Benjamin K. Maltby and Jessee Neal of Ohio for a lard lamp which uses a plunger to force the lard from the lower reservoir to the upper tube and in contact with the heat conducting wick tubes.

Description: 6½″ h., extended 9″ h., base 5½″ dia., tin, imprinted on reservoir cover "MALTBY & NEAL'S PATENT", American, ca. mid-19th century.

9-3

9-4

9-5   9-6

9-6 SWOPE PATENT

On March 13, 1860, patent No. 27,500 was issued to Zuriel Swope of Lancaster, Pennsylvania for "improvement in lamps". The patent claim covers a funnel and tubing arranged to take heat from the flame and pass it down to the lamp reservoir so that heated oil will be available to the wick.

Description: 12″ h., base 6″ dia., font 4½″ w., 2⅝″ h., 1¾″ d., shade 2¼″ dia., tin, American, ca. 19th century.

9-8 DRUMMOND CANDLE MAKER

On February 20, 1846, patent No. 4,389 was issued to John Drummond of New York for "a candle mold". A length of wicking coiled in a flat compartment hidden under the saucer base is extended through a central tubular threaded post on which a piston travels. Movement of the piston is achieved by rotating the base with respect to the reservoir. With the plunger at the bottom, the reservoir was filled with melted tallow or lard. When cold, the operation of the piston forces the tallow around the wick and extrudes a candle through the neck, which can be replenished as needed with a twist of the wrist. The drip catcher, handle and saucer base enable it to function as a candlestick. The Drummond patent was licensed to several manufacturers, one of whom was Thomas Sewell whose lard lamp (9-3) patented the following year, uses the same principle for feeding lard in a lamp.

Description: 7⅝″ h., base 6″ dia., tin, japanned, stencilled "Feb. 20th 1846 DRUMMOND PATENT T SEWELL MANUFACTURER", American, ca. 19th century.

9-5 KINNEAR PATENT

On February 4, 1851, patent No. 7,921 was issued to Delamar Kinnear of Circleville, Ohio for "improvement in lard lamps" which claims a narrow lenticular or lozenge font which keeps the fuel within thermal range of the wick tube, and a sliding cover instead of "the ordinary screw cap". It is interesting that this lamp as manufactured in large quantities by S.N. & H.C. Ufford, (7-9, p. 70), used the ordinary screw cap.

Description: 8″ h., base 5½″ dia., tin and cast iron, American, ca. 19th century.

9-7 SMITH & STONESIFER PATENT

On August 8, 1854, patent No. 11,497 was granted to Ira Smith and John Stonesifer of Boonesboro, Maryland for "improvement in lard lamps". The claim in this patent is primarily for an adjustable leather packing on the screw-actuated piston which forces the lard from the main reservoir up into proximity with the wick tube. This example was manufactured by Tilton & Sleeper of Fremont, New Hampshire.

Description: 5½″ h.o.a., base 5¾″ dia., fuel cylinder 3¾″ h., 2½″ dia., tin, japanned, stencilled "PATENTED AUGt 18th 1854", "TILTON & SLEEPER FREMONT N. HAMPSHIRE", American, ca. 19th century.

9-7   9-8

9-9　9-10

9-9　MODERATOR LAMP

The power of a heavy spring operates a piston in the cylindrical reservoir to drive a viscous fuel such as colza oil through a small central feed tube in the conventional argand type burner above. The spring was compressed by the heavy key, left, and the wick was raised by the conventional thumb wheel, right, through a rack and pinion. Invented in France in 1837 by Franchot, the moderator lamp enjoyed great popularity throughout the 19th century.

Description: 15″ h.o.a., base 5½″ dia., brass cylinder with classical figures in repousse marked "BOURDON", pewter base with brass plate marked "Tt BREVETE SANS GARANTIE DU GOUVt LAMPE MODERATEUR PERFECTIONNEE", French, ca. 19th century.

9-10　HITCHCOCK MECHANICAL LAMP

The use of a spring-driven clockwork to provide forced draft permitted a larger wick to give more light without necessity for a chimney. The lamp as shown was patented by Robert Hitchcock of Watertown, New York on December 22, 1874, incorporating a series of patented Hitchcock improvements on the original DeKeravenan patents of 1860 and 1863. The Hitchcock was the most successful of the kerosene mechanical draft lamps.

Description: 12″ h.o.a., base 5⅝″ dia., nickel-plated brass, burner deflector imprinted "HITCHCOCK LAMP WATERTOWN NEW YORK PATD FEB. 25, 1868 APL. 23, 1872 DEC. 2, 1873 JAN. 7, 1873 AUG. 12, 1873 DEC. 22, 1874", American, ca. 19th century.

9-11　HITCHCOCK FONT

This picture shows how the font was centrally supported in the lamp body so as to permit the airflow from the fan below, up around the reservoir to the burner.

Description: Left: 6″ h.o.a., font 4½″ dia., flange 5″ dia., metal strap imprinted "PATENTED NOV. 30, 1880 ROBt. HITCHCOCK, WATERTOWN N.Y.", Right: 4⅞″ dia., nickel-plated brass.

9-12　HITCHCOCK FAN AND CLOCKWORK

This is a closeup of the axial fan and clockwork assembly used in (9-10). An integral winding key is hidden by the base which has holes through which air is drawn. Lamps with centrifugal fans and wound by a removable key through a hole in the side were also made.

Description: 4″l., 1¾″ dia., brass, key 3¼″ w., cast iron.

9-11

9-12

9-13　NEWELL PATENT

On October 4, 1853, patent No. 10,099 was issued to John Newell of Boston. Since the use of fine wire mesh to prevent communication of flame had been invented by Sir Humphrey Davy in 1816, and applied to burning fluid lamps by Isaiah Jennings in 1836, Newell's claim was restricted to the silvering of the mesh to prevent corrosion, and the introduction of small vent holes in the burner caps to prevent bursting due to the buildup of pressure within the font.

Description: 9½" h.o.a., base 4⅜" dia., burner unit 3½" l., ⅞" dia., burner marked "PATENT APPLIED FOR", pewter, American, ca. 19th century.

9-13

9-14

9-14　HORSFORD & NICHOLS PATENT

On October 30, 1855, patent No. 13,729 was issued to E. N. Horsford and James R. Nichols of Massachusetts. Their lamp also utilized the wire gauze feature for safety but the patent claim covered an inner safety wick tube which was barbed to hold the wick in place.

Description: 6" h., 3¾" dia., pattern glass, tin burner marked "PATENT APPLIED FOR", American, ca. 19th century.

9-15　BELL'S PATENT

On November 14, 1854, patent No. 11,928 was granted to William Bell of Boston. Since most explosions occurred from attempts to refill a fluid lamp while lighted, Bell provided a separate filler chamber that did not require removal of the burner. Safety was still achieved by the use of Davy's wire gauze at the bottom of the chamber.

Description: 10¼" h.o.a., base 3½" sq., glass, blown and pressed, American, ca. 19th century.

9-15

9-16　STAR TUMBLER LAMP PATENT

The Star Tumbler lamp patented January 13, 1874, consists of an ordinary drinking tumbler equipped with a small tin lamp removable by the attached wire rod. A tin strap supports the bail handle and the hinged tin chimney. The burner turnup is marked "E. Miller and Co., Meriden, Conn.", and in one other example, the glass is marked "Taylor Mfg. Co., New Britain, Conn."

Description: 5¾" h.o.a., bail 4½" l., tumbler 3½" h., 3¼" dia., chimney 1¾" h., 2" w., embossed "STAR PATENTED JAN 13 1874 TUMBLER", tin lamp 1" h., 2⅛" dia., brass burner marked "E. MILLER and CO. MERIDEN.—CONN.", American, ca. 19th century.

9-16

9-17

9-17   SARGENT'S PATENT

On March 4, 1856, patent No. 14,369 was issued to Prentice Sargent of Newburyport, Massachusetts for "improvement in lamps for burning rosin oil". This is basically a form of argand lamp designed to prevent smoking caused by any gusts of air. In common with many other rosin oil burners, a central deflector button directs air to the inside of the annular wick.

Description: 9″ h.o.a., base 4⅜″ dia., burner marked "SARGENT'S PATENT MAR 4 1856", glass and brass, American, ca. 19th century.

9-18

9-18   DAVIS PATENT

On May 6, 1856, patent No. 14,806 was granted to Samuel Davis of Pennsylvania for a lard lamp. At first glance, Davis appears to have reinvented the Argand lamp but with three new features. He claims that the light can be extinguished by holding the thumb against the single aperture near the base, excluding air to the center of the wick. He also uses two flat wicks in a cone-shaped feeder to form a complete circle, and claims that one wick can be retracted to diminish the light and conserve fuel.

Description: 7″ h.o.a., base 5¾″ dia., tin, japanned, stenciled "SAML DAVIS" PATENTED MAY 6 1856", American, ca. 19th century.

9-19   GREENE PATENT

On April 21, 1857, patent No. 17,086 was issued to Dr. Charles A. Greene of Philadelphia. In his patent, Greene claims a small auxiliary wick to heat the burner sufficiently to generate a flammable gas from the volatile fluid after which the ignited gas provides sufficient heat for vaporization. Most examples did not incorporate the auxiliary burner. The gas which is emitted through several small horizontal holes in the burner can be adjusted by the knurled button at the top of the burner.

Description: 8″ h.o.a., base 3¾″ dia., burner 7″ l., brass disc 1½″ dia., marked "DR. C.A. GREENE PATENT APRIL 21 1857", glass and brass, American, ca. 19th century.

9-20   PERKINS AND HOUSE PATENT

On December 11, 1866, patent No. 60,416 was issued to J. M. Perkins and M. W. House of Cleveland, Ohio for a non-explosive lamp. During the first decade of kerosene lighting, much of the fuel was adulterated with volatile components such as naptha or benzine, resulting in all of the hazards associated with burning fluids. Perkins & House produced a safe lamp by incorporating three important features: the lamp being made of metal was unbreakable, an auxiliary filler opening permitted filling the lamp while lighted, and cool air from below was directed between the reservoir and the central font to the burner, providing air cooling to the fuel supply.

Description: 9½″ h.o.a., base 4½″ dia., font marked "PERKINS & HOUSE SAFETY LAMP CLEV'D. NON-EXPLOSIVE LAMP Co. CLEVELAND & NEW YORK", "PAT'D NOV. 24, 1857 DEC. 11, 1866 NOV. 18, 1871", Burner marked "E. MILLER & CO., MERIDEN CONN.", spun brass, American, ca. 19th century.

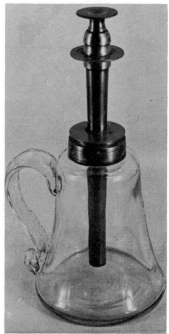

9-19

9-20

CHAPTER X

SPECIAL PURPOSE LAMPS

Most lamps and candles were intended for use as general lighting. In many cases, however, light was used to "look at" rather than to "see by".

Light has been an important part of nearly all religious observances, and many lamps have been designed for this specific purpose.

The excitement and fervor of political campaigns were for many years enhanced by the torchlight parade, and since long before Paul Revere's time, lights have been used for signaling.

Since light adds hours to the working day, it is not surprising that time lamps were developed to provide the added service of telling time.

The traveler had special needs for small collapsible pocket lights to carry with him, and each form of transportation had its own special requirements that were satisfied by ingenious designs.

Small long burning lamps giving little light were useful for night-lights, and to maintain a small flame when needed.

LENS

10-1

10-1 LENS CANDLEHOLDER

Glass lenses were often applied to lamps though seldom to candles, to increase the illumination over a limited critical area. A most unusual arragement is the adjustable feature that permits the location of the spot to be controlled. A sand-weighted base counterbalances the heavy glass lens.

Description: 13½″ h., base 4⅞″ sq., lens 2⅝″ dia., tin, marked "FINCHETT JUNE 7 1889 FLEET ST. LONDON", English, ca. 19th century.

10-2

10-2 DOUBLE LENS LAMP

This "lamp" is really a tin holder for a glass whale oil lamp and two lenses. To secure maximum benefit from the lens, the plane of the burner should be parallel to the plane of the lens. In this case, the glass lamp may be rotated in the holder.

Description: 10¾″ h., base 4½″ dia., lens 3″ dia., glass font 2½″ h., 1⅞″ dia., tin, black japanned, American, ca. 1830.

10-3 DOUBLE LENS LAMP

The use of a drum-shaped font provides an ample fuel reservoir while still permitting the short focal length lens to be properly positioned.

Description: 9½″ h., base 3½″ dia., pewter, American, ca. early 19th century.

10-4 MULTIPLE LENS LAMP

In this example, four lenses provide light for four people from a single twin-burner whale oil lamp. A cast iron base provides the necessary stability. Here, the forty-five degree position of the wick tubes assures equal light to all positions.

Description: 9″ h., base 4″ dia., lens 3″ dia., tin, japanned, iron base painted, American, ca. 1820.

10-3

10-4

BULLS EYE

10-5   DARK LANTERN

Lenses applied to lanterns are useful for directionally increasing the amount of illumination, or the useful range when used for signaling. Rotation of an inner cylinder acts as a shutter; single wick whale oil lamp provides light.

Description: 6¼″ h., 1½″ dia., lens 3¼″ l., 1½″ w., tin, American, ca. 19th century.

10-6   TRIPLE BULLS EYE LANTERN

The three bulls eyes on this early lantern while decorative in appearance provide little, if any lens effect.

Description: 5″ h., 2⅝″ sq., tin, French, ca. 1700.

10-5   *10-6*

10-7   PATTERNED LENS LANTERNS

As in these examples, patterned lenses were used primarily for decorative effect. They were undoubtedly more rugged than flat glass windows but their lens value would be limited by the amount of configuration. Both lanterns contain whale oil lamps.

Description: Left: 5¾″ h., 3″ w., 8-pointed star lens 2⅜″ dia., Right: 5¾″ h., 2¾″ w., 18-lobe sunburst oval lens 3¼″ h., 2½″ w., both half-round, tin, American, ca. 1830.

10-8   LENS LANTERN

This hand lantern with unique built-in lighter mechanism has a large well formed lens that is highly effective. The cluster of small air holes at the bottom insures efficient combustion.

Description: 5¾″ h., tin, American, ca. 19th century.

10-7

10-8

10-9   *10-10*

10-9   CARDAN TIME INDICATING LAMP

Raised Roman numerals from V to IIII on pewter straps indicate the passage of nighttime hours with the consumption of fuel. Unlike (10-11) and (10-12), in this style of time lamp, sometimes known to collectors as a "Nuremburg" lamp, the font is ideally located to be easily read by the light of the lamp itself.

Description: 10″ h.o.a., base 4″ dia., ribbed glass font 3″ h., 2½″ dia., pewter and glass, European, ca. 1700.

10-10   CARDAN TIME INDICATING LAMP

The cylindrical shaped font has an advantage over (10-9) in that the Roman numerals are evenly spaced. The extra handle on the removable reservoir of this example facilitates filling.

Description: 15″ h., base 7″ dia., pewter and glass, German, ca. 1750.

10-11   GRAND VAL'S TIME INDICATING LAMP

King Alfred is credited with marking a candle to indicate the passage of time. As late as 1881, a patent was issued for a small kerosene time indicating night light. In this example, the tubular column font is graduate from "8" to "6" to indicate the passage of the nighttime hours, as the fuel is consumed.

Description: 8″ h.o.a., column font 5″ h., marked with numerals 8 to 6, reverse column marked with an eagle, base 2⅝″ dia., marked "GRAND-VAL'S PERFECT INDICATOR", under base marked "PAT'D 1881", blue glass shade, American, ca. 19th century.

10-12   PRIDE OF AMERICA TIME INDICATING LAMP

Similar in principle to (10-11), is the Pride of America lamp. Since the accuracy of these lamps depended on the quality of the fuel as well as the setting of the wick, their value was probably limited to medication in the sickroom.

Description: 6⅞″ h.o.a., column font 4″ h., marked with numerals 8 to 5, with 6 marked on top of base, base 2⅝″ dia., marked "TIME & LIGHT, PRIDE OF AMERICA GRAND VAL'S PERFECT INDICATING LAMP", under base marked "PAT APLD FOR", milk glass shade, American, ca. 19th century.

10-11   *10-12*

86

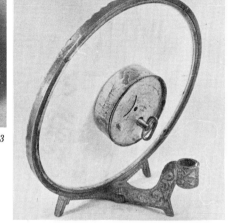

10-13

10-14

10-13 ILLUMINATED CLOCK

Unlike the time lamp that depends upon the unpredictable rate of fuel consumption for its accuracy, this standard spring driven clock with translucent glass dial relies upon the lamp (or gaslight) solely for illumination. Its accuracy would be as good as its clockwork.

Description: Front view shows clock dial 5¾″ dia.o.a., back view shows one-day lever action Waterbury clock 2″ dia., marked inside "Patented Dec 23 90, Jan 12 91 made in U.S.A.", brass and translucent glass, American, ca. 19th century.

10-14 BENSEL PATENT CLOCK LAMP

As in the lamp shown here, invented by Peter C. Bensel, clockworks were adapted in various ways to rotate a translucent glass cylinder around a small night light. A stationary pointer indicates the time.

Description: 11″ h., base 4″ dia., marked "P.C. BENSEL, N.Y. PATENTED MAY 14 1872 AND JULY 7 1885", milk glass cylinder 4¾″ dia., kerosene lamp dia. 3¾″, brass, glass, American, ca. 19th century.

10-15 ILLUMINATED ALARM CLOCK

The tripping mechanism of this otherwise conventional alarm clock is arranged to strike a wooden match on a strip of sandpaper and apply it to the wick of a small lamp.

Description: Front and rear views show lamp slid into position with wick tube extending above the top in line with the sulphur tipped match, label with directions for setting and regulating imprinted "MANUFACTURED BY H.J. DAVIES SUCCESSOR TO G.A. JONES CO., 1858 NO. 5 CORTLAND St., NEW YORK", American, ca. 19th century.

10-15

RELIGIOUS OR CEREMONIAL

10-16

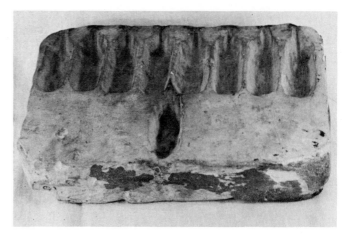

10-17

10-16   HANUKAH LIGHT

The observance of Hanukah, the Jewish
Festival of Lights, requires a special lamp
having eight candles or oil receptacles
plus the Shammash, a special receptacle
from which the others were lighted. In this
ancient example, the Shammash is in the
center.

Description: 1″ h., 4¾″ w., center 1½″ dia.,
sandstone, Egyptian, ca. 2nd century, A.D.

10-17   HANUKAH LAMP

A very primitive Hanukah lamp hollowed
out of sandstone. The receptacle in the
foreground is the Shammash.

Description: 1¾″ h., 7½″ l., 4¾″ w., sandstone, Yemen, ca. 1600.

10-18   HANUKAH LAMP

This elaborate pewter Hanukah lamp has the Shammash
or server on the upper right. Cylinder on left is
representative of the Torah, the sacred scrolls. A narrow
drip tray under the eight lamps conducts any dripped oil
to the two small cups on either side.

Description: 10″ h.o.a., 10″ l., pewter, German, ca. 1820.

10-19   HANUKAH LAMP

This graceful lamp resembles a Menorah
in construction but the eight lamps
instead of seven, and the presence of a
Shammash in front identify it as a
Hanukah. All lamps contain wick supports.

Description: 11½″ h., 9″ w., base 4½″ dia.,
brass.

10-18

10-19

10-20

10-20   ROLLING BALL LAMP

Two pierced brass hemispheres enclose a triple gimbal support for a small oil lamp. Most of these lamps are variously attributed to far Eastern countries, and are believed by many to have been used in observance of wedding rites.

Description: 9½" dia., brass, probably India.

10-21   HINDU VOTIVE LAMP

This representation of the Hindu goddess "Lakshmi Dipavali" standing on a small pedestal supports an open saucer lamp.

Description: 11" h., base 2½" sq., brass, one of a pair, South India, ca. 1700.

10-21

10-22   FESTIVE LAMPS

Cup shaped lamps of colored glass were used for decoration during the Christmas holiday season. Float wicks with oil were often used but an ingenious tripod wick support with hooked handle is used in the green lamp on left, and a vigil candle was often used in the diamond pattern type on the right.

Description: Left: 3" h., 2½" dia., glass, Lower left: metal wick holder, Right: 3½" h., 2¼" dia., glass, ca. 19th century.

10-23   CHRISTMAS TREE CANDLEHOLDERS

At the top are three forms of counterweighted candleholders designed to hang on the branches of a Christmas tree. A home made example in center has a wire bent to form a pricket and a counterweight of lead. The three holders at the bottom are fastened on the tree by spring clips.

10-22

Description: Top left: 5" l., 1¼" dia., painted clay ball, Center: 5½" l., iron wire, lead weight, Right: 6" l., 1⅞" dia., faceted white metal, lacquered in transparent colors, holder 1" dia., tin, Lower left: 2½" l., 1¼" dia., lacquered tin, Center: 1½" l., ¾" w., lacquered tin, Right: 1¾" l., 1¼" dia., lacquered tin, ca. 19th century.

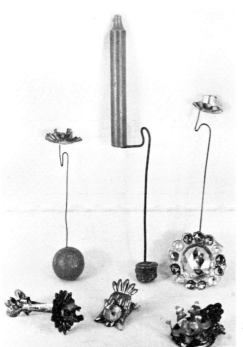

10-23

10-24   ALTAR CANDLEHOLDER

The slender central column and unusual height of this graceful holder is typical of many early altar candleholders. The four components are crudely threaded together.

Description: 22" h., base 8" dia., drip pan 3" dia., brass, ca. 16th century.

10-24

CAMPAIGN

10-25

10-26

10-25   CAMPAIGN CAP TORCH

A small nickel-plated torch supported by a wire trunnion is fastened to the crown of this campaign parader's cap, quite possibly used by a member of a band.

Description: Torch 3½″ h., 2¾″ dia., nickel, cap white oilcloth, grey crown, black visor, American, ca. 1868.

10-26   STAR CAMPAIGN TORCH

The drum shaped oil reservoir is decorated with five pyramidal points; the torch is supported by the usual off-center trunnion mounting.

Description: 5″ dia., points each 1½″ l., tin painted with red star in center on white, circled in blue, American, ca. 19th century.

10-27

10-27   BALLOT BOX TORCH

A spherical glass reservoir, resembling a globe ballot box is secured between the upper and lower tin plates by four tin posts. It was patented by J. McGregor Adams, Chicago, Illinois.

Description: Frame 4″ h., 4½″ sq., glass font imprinted "A & W Mfg. Co. Chicago Pat Jan 27-80", tin and glass, American, ca. 19th century.

10-28   BEAVER HAT TORCH

The tin reservoir of this torch was fashioned in the form of a beaver hat. Tin buttons soldered to the sides provide the trunnion mount similar to the bail handles on tin pails. The wire trunnion is attached to a tin socket for receiving a wood pole.

Description: Crown 3½″ h., 4½″ dia., brim 6¼″ x 4¼″, tin, marked underneath "PAT APPLD FOR", probably used in James Buchanan campaign, American, ca. 19th century.

10-28

10-29 TRIANGULAR CAMPAIGN LANTERN

Square or triangular tin lanterns with glass panes on which translucent pictures or slogans could be mounted were popular during the Lincoln campaign of 1864. In the two views of this example, one side, a picture of Lincoln is a lithograph by Louis Prang of Boston; the second side reads "Union and Liberty", the third side, not shown, reads "Lincoln and Johnson". A candle was the source of illumination.

Description: Tin frame with glass panels ea. 6¼″ h., 8″ w., imprint at bottom of Lincoln picture "ABRAHAM LINCOLN" "LITHOGRAPH BY LOUIS PRANG 1861 — L. PRANG & CO. 4 MERCHANTS ROW, BOSTON", American, ca. 19th century.

10-29

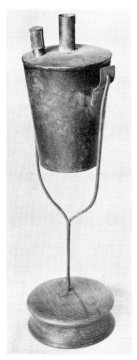

10-30

10-31 SQUARE CAMPAIGN LANTERN

A fine degree of craftsmanship for a campaign lantern is evident in this example which uses colored and decorated glass in the windows, leaf perforations in the tin frame, and brass hood over the chimney. A tin lamp with brass burning fluid burner and cap is held stationary with tin flanges. The location of the trunnion mounting on the corners instead of sides, is also unusual.

Description: 9″ h.o.a., 5″ sq., glass inserts 3⅝″ dia., blue, red, and etched pattern, American, ca. 19th century.

10-30 TIN CAMPAIGN TORCH

This design is unusual for a campaign torch in having a separate filler tube with tight fitting cover. The offset tin ears illustrate another arrangement for trunnion mounting.

Description: 13″ h.o.a., top 4″ dia., bottom 3″ dia., tin, with wire bail, American, ca. 19th century.

10-31

TRAVEL

10-32 WHIPPLE TRAVEL LIGHT

Small personal lights which the traveler could use at his destination appear in various forms. One of the neatest is the Whipple patent which not only carried its own taper and socket but also a receptacle for matches and convenient striking plate.

Description: 3½″ l., ¾″ w., ½″ d., tin, black japanned, scratcher on top imprinted "WHIPPLE'S PATENT MAY 28, 1867 TAPERS SOLD AT 297 WAS'N ST. BOSTON", American, ca. 19th century.

10-32

10-33

10-33 TRAVEL CANDLESTICK

The twin saucers, one with threaded stud, screw together to carry the candle sockets. This design is found in wood, metal and leather covered brass, and some examples also contain an extinguisher or inkwell.

Description: 5″ dia., brass, English, ca. 19th century.

10-34 MINOR'S FOLDING LANTERN

This ingenious device only ¾″ thick, opens into a candle lantern complete with two mica windows and bright tin reflector. A compartment for spare candles and matches as well as a match scratcher are provided. The pivoted candleholder serves to lock the lantern in its opened position. The same basic design appeared in World War I as government issue.

Description: Left: 5⅛″ h., 3″ w., ¾″ thick, stencilled "MINOR'S PATENT JAN. 24th 1865", Right: open, 5⅛″ h., sides 3⅝″ w., tin, japanned brown, American, ca. 19th century.

10-34

10-35

10-35 THE READY LIGHT

The tin pocket case carries four small "self-lighting" candles which can be mounted on a small wire pricket holder attached to the case. The wick terminates in a matchhead.

Description: 2″ sq., ¾″ d., tin enamelled "THE READY LIGHT" "PATENTED JULY 28 1885" "PORTLAND, ME. U.S.A.", American, ca. 19th century.

10-36

10-36   TRAVELING LAMP

The non-spillable characteristics of the candle made it popular for travel lights. However, Yankee ingenuity rose to the challenge in this cleverly designed whale oil lamp with a cork which effectively seals the burner and reservoir.

Description: Closed and complete 3¾″ h., 1 3/16″ dia., Left: lower cylinder with whale oil burner, Right: cylinder with compartment for sealing wax or wafers, tin, blue japanned, cover with label "J. HATCH PATENT BOSTON", American, ca. 19th century.

10-38   WATCH POCKET LAMP

Pressure on the stem causes the rotation of a disc carrying a number of small friction igniters that light the wick. The small size of the reservoir limited its practical use to that of a match for striking a light, or as a lamp for very intermittent use.

Description: Case marked "Watch Pocket Lamp-Fulmer & Schwing Mfg. Co., N.Y.,-Pat. June 23, July 21, 91", American, ca. 19th century.

10-38

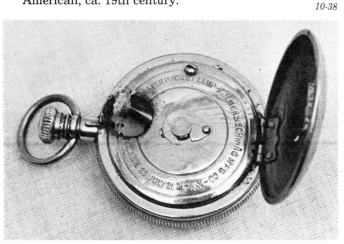

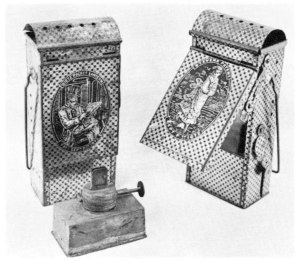

10-37

10-37   STEVENS TRAVEL LANTERN

Although not collapsible like (10-34), the shallow design and hinged door qualify this as a travel light. A small pivoted access door and extension thumbwheel permit lighting and adjustment without disassembly.

Description: 5¾″ h., 2¾″ w., 1½″ d., tin, printed gold with black transfer patterns, patented by John Stevens, Orange, New Jersey, Sept. 7, 1875, American, ca. 19th century.

10-39

10-39   CANE LIGHT

A pushup taper holder is the feature of this silver cane handle.

Description: 4″ l., 1¼″ dia., silver, American, ca. 19th century.

10-40

10-40   PEDESTRIAN TRAVEL LAMP

The traveler enroute often required specialized lighting depending on his mode of transportation. This versatile lantern with telescoping chimney, whale oil lamp with wick pick, a spill proof cap (stored on outside fitting) and polished tin reflector, was ideally suited to the pedestrian. Folding handles on rear and a sharpened wire hook permit use as a hand lantern or to be worn. A wire loop and flat base permit suspension or table use.

Description: 3¾″ h., as shown, 3″ h. closed, 2″ dia., brass, American, ca. early 19th century.

10-42   BICYCLE LAMP

A seven-position spring loaded valve on the top of the reservoir controls the injection of water to the lower chamber containing calcium carbide to produce acetylene gas. Precision beam control is provided by a large efficient aluminum reflector without the use of a lens.

Description: 6″ h., 5″ d., lens 3″ dia., brass nickel-plated, pantograph bracket, marked "GERMANY", ca. 19th century.

10-42

10-41

10-41   BICYCLE LAMP

The Hitchcock Lamp Company, in addition to mechanical lamp (9-10, p. 80), produced this "Happy Thought" kerosene bicycle lamp. The shockproof pantograph mounting bracket is equipped with a precision aiming device and an external wick control for adjustment by the cyclist. One of the small colored side windows slides open for lighting the wick.

Description: 6″ h., base 3¼″ dia., lens 3″ dia., side windows red and green, ¾″ h., ⅝″ w., nickel, imprinted "HITCH-COCK LAMP CO. MANUFACTURERS WATERTOWN N.Y." "HAPPY THOUGHT", American, ca. late 19th century.

10-43   BICYCLE LAMP

A half inch wick and polished reflector team up with a double convex lens to provide a controlled beam in this kerosene bicycle lamp which resembles a small carriage lamp in design.

Description: 6″ h., 3″ d., lens 2¼″ dia., nickel-plated brass, stamped on back "TALLY-HO", on bottom "MADE IN UNITED STATES OF AMERICA PAT APPLIED FOR THE BRIDGEPORT GUN IMPLEMENT CO. BRIDGEPORT, CONN.", American, ca. 19th century.

10-43

10-44

10-45 TRUNNION LAMP

Although not as effective as a full gimbal, the trunnion mount is useful for shipboard application. A small hanging ring permits use as a wall bracket.

Description: 7″ h., base 5″ dia., pewter, brass camphine burner with extinguisher caps, American, ca. 19th century.

10-45

10-44 GIMBAL LAMP

Full gimbal mounting compensated for the roll of a ship in heavy weather. Maximum stability is provided to the tin font by a heavy ballast weight in the bottom. The saucer base is equipped with a hanging ring to permit wall mounting.

Description: 3⅜″ h., base 6″ dia., font 4″ dia., tin, painted black, brass whale oil burner, American, ca. 19th century.

10-47 MARINE LANTERN

Ships' running and signal lights pose the most rigid requirements in terms of rugged dependability. A heavy brass lantern and bail support a glass globe protected by a heavy wire guard. The kerosene burner inserted through the bottom is held by flat spring catches.

Description: 15″ h., 7″ dia., globe 5½″ h., 6″ dia., brass, wt. 8 lbs., American, ca. 1865.

10-46 DOUBLE POINTED CANDLEHOLDER

Although used in many other applications, the double pointed candleholder was exceptionally useful in lading the hold of a ship since it could be stuck into the top or side of the cargo, or the frame of the ship.

Description: 7″ h.o.a., 4″ w., socket 3¼″ l., 1¼″ dia., wrought iron, American, ca. 19th century.

10-46

10-47

TRANSPORTATION

RICKSHAW

10-48

CANDLE—COACH

10-49

10-48   RICKSHAW LANTERN

More decorative than utilitarian, this delicately pierced brass lantern was probably adequate to mark the progress of a rickshaw. The flame of the small whale oil type burner is protected by a conical glass globe which is supported by five separate crudely threaded sections of the frame which screw together.

Description: 7″ h., 3″ dia., brass, Japanese.

10-49   COACH LIGHT

The spring loaded candleholder is ideally suited to this carriage lamp, insuring that the flame is always centered for both the round beveled window (left) in front and the red bulls-eye taillight in the rear. A beveled plate glass window on the side makes use of otherwise wasted light.

Description: 12″ h., 4″ dia., side glass 3¾″ h., 4¾″ w., lens 5½″ dia., brass, painted black, nickel-plated trim, American, ca. 19th century.

KEROSENE—COACH

10-50

BUGGY

10-51

10-50   COACH LAMP

In this example, a small kerosene lamp, removable through the rear door provides the illumination.

Description: 11″ h., oval lens 4½″ x 5½″, beveled glass 3½″ x 4½″, brass, painted black, polished surfaces nickel-plated brass, burner marked "E. MILLER & CO. - MADE IN USA", American, early 20th century.

10-51   BUGGY LIGHT

The functional design of this early kerosene buggy lamp utilizes the cylindrical body later used in auto lamps. A highly polished parabolic silvered reflector directs a beam through the heavy beveled plate glass door. The kerosene lamp is inserted through the bottom.

Description: 11″ h., 5″ dia., 5″ d., sheet iron, painted black, copper plate on side "WHITE MFG. CO. BRIDGEPORT, CONN. PATENTED FEB 10 1874, REISSUED MAR 6, 1877", American, ca. 19th century.

10-52   AUTO LAMP

The influence of carriage lamp design is obvious in this early kerosene lamp for the horseless carriage.

Description: 10″ h., 4¼″ cube center, round and sq. glass side, polished nickel reflector opposite round glass, sheet iron, painted black, brass top marked "E & J-DETROIT, MICH. PAT. DEC. 9, 1908", American, ca. 20th century.

10-54   AUTO LAMP

Strictly functional, this no-nonsense Dietz driving lamp is equipped with a glass roundel mounted in a polished brass hinged bezel. Small holes in the rear of the internal aluminum reflector provide light for the red bulls eye. The kerosene lamp is inserted through the bottom.

Description: 11½″ h., body 4½″ dia., 6½″ d., sheet iron, painted black, brass bezel 6¼″ dia., marked "DIETZ UNION DRIVING LAMP — NEW YORK — USA — PATENTED JAN 25, 97, JAN. 2, 08, SEPT. 25, 06, JAN. 22, 07", American, ca. 20th century.

10-52

10-53

10-53   AUTO LAMP

Internal silvered reflecting surfaces and a large beveled lens assure high efficiency. The cylindrical body necessitates a costly curved window, and a small red bulls eye is mounted in the hinged rear access door. The kerosene lamp screws through the bottom.

Description: 11″ h., 6″ dia., 7″ d., lens 6″ dia., sheet iron, painted black with nickel-plated brass, marked on inside back "GRAY AND DAVIS", American, ca. 20th century.

10-55   AUTO MARKER LIGHTS

The Ford Model T dashboard light on the right with the white Fresnel lens in the bottom hinged door matches the red tail light on the left which, however, has a white side window to light the license plate.

The kerosene lamp attaches through the bottom by means of a bayonet fitting.

Description: 4″ h., 3½″ dia., 5″ d., lenses 4″ dia., sheet iron, painted black, marked "EDMUNDS AND JONES MFG. CO. DETROIT, MICH. MODEL 8-FORD", bottom of lamp font marked "E & J NO.3-414 PAT. MAY 26-14, JUNE 23-14", American, ca. 20th century.

10-54

10-55

10-56 RAILROAD LANTERN

Railroad crews required a rugged dependable lantern, both for illumination as well as for signaling. A sturdy wire guard protects the globe from breakage. The thumbscrew clamp permits removal of the top if globe replacement should become necessary. The glass whale oil lamp is inserted through the bottom.

Description: 12″ h., 6½″ dia., lamp font 3″ dia., sheet iron, American, ca. 1860.

10-57 PRESENTATION LANTERN

Special presentation lanterns were often embellished with the owner's name. This globe is decorated with etchings of locomotive, oil can, flare and horseshoe marked "Good Luck" and containing a crossed hammer and monkey wrench. The kerosene lamp used a flat wick.

Description: 11¼″ h., 5¼″ dia., globe 5″ h., 4½″ dia., brass, marked "WM PORTER'S SONS, N.Y. PATD APR 29,67 AUG. 3,69 JUNE 13,71", American, ca. 19th century.

10-56

10-57

10-58 RAILROAD LANTERN

Unlike the presentation piece, most railroad lanterns were the property of the railroad and were often marked with the road's initials — in this case "B & A R. R." for the Boston & Albany Railroad. The glass kerosene lamp is removable through the bottom by means of a bayonet joint.

Description: 10″ h., 4″ dia., tin, glass globe marked "B & A R R", burner marked "E. MILLER & CO. MERIDEN CONN. — BEACON — PATENTED APR. 19,1875 MAR. 21,1876", Top cap marked "STEAM GAUGE AND LANTERN CO., SYRACUSE, N.Y.", American, ca. 19th century.

10-59 PRESENTATION LANTERN

This presentation lantern, engraved "A. McShaw" in Old English in a leafy oval wreath, has a patented hinged brass door containing a polished concave reflector four inches in diameter. The brass kerosene lamp is inserted through the bottom and held by flat spring clips.

Description: 12″ h., base 6⅛″ dia., glass globe 5″ dia., marked "LINDLEY EXCELSIOR, PATENT JUNE 2,1863", brass, American, ca. 19th century.

10-58

10-59

10-60 PRESENTATION LANTERN

"K. MUNSON" was the lucky recipient of this silverplated presentation piece. In addition to the owner's name engraved within a decorated rectangle, the top two and a quarter inches of the globe is flashed with green glass to reduce glare when used for illumination. The silver-plated kerosene lamp screws in through the bottom.

Description: 10″ h., base 5″ dia., globe 5″ h., 4″ dia., silverplated, marked on bottom "ADAMS PATENTED APR 26,64 CHICAGO ILL", American, ca. 19th century.

10-62 PRESENTATION LANTERN

This "railroad" lantern, equipped with a double whale oil burner, was used by "J. W. PATTERSON" agent for Sanford's line of steam packets plying between Maine's Penobscot River ports and Boston during the last half of the nineteenth century.

Description: 11″ h., glass globe 4½″ dia., engraved "J. W. PATTERSON AGENT SANFORD'S LINE", brass, nickel-plated, marked under side of base "J. H. KELLY ROCHESTER", American, ca. 19th century.

10-60

10-61

10-61 CONDUCTOR'S LANTERN

"W.C. PATTISON" was the proud owner of this Blake's patent conductor's armhole lantern equipped with a two-wick whale oil burner.

Description: 15⅜″ h.o.a., base 5¾″ dia., armhole 4″ dia., glass globe 6″ h., 4⅞″ dia., brass with black finish, marked "BLAKES PATENT JAN'Y 13, 1859", American, ca. 19th century.

10-63 RAILROAD CAR LIGHT

The familiar spring loaded candleholder in a more rugged design and equipped with a small glass chimney has been adapted to wall bracket mounting for use in parlor car lighting.

Description: 9½″ h.o.a., 2½″ dia., copper, marked "THE SAFETY CO. NEW YORK", American, ca. 19th century.

10-62

10-63

10-64

10-64   FAIRY NIGHT LIGHT

Originally designed by Samuel Clarke as a night light using his wax candles, the two piece Fairy lamp was made by many glasshouses in untold combinations of patterns and colors. In addition to the use of single lamps in the bedroom., quantities were used for decorative purposes on festive occasions.

Description: 5¾" h., 4" dia., ribbon glass, pink, white, green (Nailsea) with Clarke's pressed glass base, ca. 19th century.

10-66

10-65

10-65   CLARKE'S NIGHT CANDLES

Clarke's Pyramid Night Lights labelled "the burglar's horror" were made to "burn Nine hours each". In addition to use in Fairy lamps, they were intended for Clarke's Pyramid Food Warmer for use in the nursery. In the lower right is a small porcelain saucer in which the candle was burned.

Description: Unopened box 5⅛" l., 3½" w., 3" h., label in colors marked "CLARKE'S PYRAMID NIGHT LIGHTS", Foreground: candle 1½" h., 1⅝" dia., saucer 2⅜" dia., black transfer "FOR CLARKE'S PATENT PYRAMID NIGHT LIGHTS", England, ca. 19th century.

10-66   GLOW LAMP

Like the Fairy lamp, this miniature night light provides a soft lighted decoration rather than bright illumination and comes in many shape and color combinations. The small patented burner shown in foreground claims "100 hours light for one cent" and one filling of kerosene was said to burn two hundred hours.

Description: 5" h.o.a., globe 2½" dia., base 4" dia., milk glass with painted flowers, Patented Aug. 27,1895, American, ca. 19th century.

10-67   CIGAR LIGHTER

Many small lamps were called upon to light cigars but this example was designed expressly for this purpose and includes a convenient cigar cutter mounted on the front. To provide heat rather than light, alcohol was the fuel and therefore needed the small cap to prevent evaporation when not in use.

Description: 7" h., copper, pewter and brass, ca. 1900.

CIGAR LIGHTER

10-67

CHAPTER XI

LIGHTS
TO
WORK BY

The short days of winter did not provide enough hours for many of the early craftsmen and tradesmen, and some industries such as mining could not be carried on in daylight at all. For most tasks, no unusual lighting devices were required but the special needs of certain trades called for specific solutions in providing artificial light.

Some of these work lights were quite obviously designed for one particular occupation while others, especially if their objective was to concentrate light or provide heat, were used by various artisans having common requirements. It is risky therefore, to attribute lamps in this latter category too precisely to a single specific trade.

In addition to the tradesman, the various arts and professions often involved special considerations in the design of lighting devices, some of which are included in the following pages.

MINERS' LAMPS

11-1

11-1 MINER'S LAMP

The familiar Betty lamp design in this example has been fabricated of heavy cast iron as were most early miners' lights to withstand the physical abuse associated with that occupation. The extremely heavy hook is also typical of most miners' lamps.

Description: 4½″ l., 1¾″ h., 3¼″ w., cast iron, face plate 1½″ h., 2″ w., brass, American.

11-3 MINER'S LAMP

This is another cast iron Betty type miner's lamp with an unusual circular reservoir. Although most of these early cast iron miners' lights are attributed to Germany or central Europe, as might be expected, many are found in Pennsylvania.

Description: 4½″ dia., cast iron, German.

11-2

11-2 MINER'S LAMP

This familiar type of cast iron miner's light, more commonly found with a circular font, supported by a heavy trunnion mount attached to a long hooked rod by means of a swivel joint, is embellished with a brass rooster.

Description: 7½″ h., 5½″ w., cast iron and brass, marked "OLLAGNO — A. GIETIENNE LOIRS", French.

11-4 MINER'S SAFETY LAMP

Many variations of this lamp which employs the Davy principle of using a wire gauze to prevent transmission of flame were manufactured in Europe and the United States. This improved version incorporates a heavy glass cylinder for better light and is equipped with a built-in wickpick and extinguisher which can be operated without opening the lamp.

Description: 10¼″ h., base 3½″ dia., 4″ h., brass and glass, marked "AMERICAN SAFETY LAMP — MINE SUPPLY CO., SCRANTON, PA.", American.

11-3

11-4

11-5

11-6

11-5   MINER'S CAP LAMP

This small lamp with a big wick is typical of many different designs of miners' cap lamps. The font in this example of a coffeepot shape, is also found frequently in a milk can design, always with a large wick tube and hinged cover. This type of lamp as well as the sticking tommy, (11-7, 11-8), is listed in the Sears Roebuck catalogs of the early twentieth century.

Description: 2″ h., base 1⅝″ dia., top 1¼″ dia., tin, marked "LIBERTY C.L.ANTON MFGR. & PATENTEE MONONGAHELA CITY WASHINGTON CO. PA.", American, ca. early 20th century.

11-6   MINER'S LAMP CAP

Many more cap lamps seem to have survived than the caps themselves. This picture clearly shows how the little lamp was worn by the miner. Both cap and lamps are shown in Sears Roebuck catalog for 1902.

Description: Cap — brown duck, American, ca. 20th century.

11-7   MINER'S CANDLESTICK

The familiar "Sticking Tommy" provided the miner with a handy candleholder that could be worn on the cap or stuck in a timber or wall of the mine. The cast aluminum handle of this example contains a matchbox with sliding cover.

Description: 11½″ l.o.a., socket ¾″ dia., handle 3½″ l., 2″ w., steel and cast aluminum, American.

11-8   MINER'S CANDLESTICK

The hook and spike on this miner's stick patented by Hugh L. Rice, Fair Play, Colorado, fold back into the handle to make it safe and small enough to carry in the pocket when not in use. The spring socket grips the candle securely.

Description: 6½″ l., folded 4″ l., steel, marked ″RICE PAT. MAR. 29, '81″, American, 19th century.

11-7

11-8

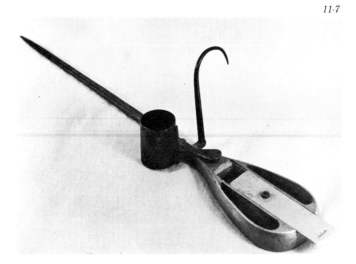

103

SHOP LAMPS

11-9

11-9   PIG LAMP

About the only thing that can be said with certainty regarding the pig lamp is that it consists of a horizontal tin cylinder with three large wick tubes and sometimes a filler tube with a cork. Often the tube caps, handle and "tray" shown in this example, are also found. It is usually agreed that these were shop lamps but no real evidence indicates whether they were for light or heat.

Description: 9″ l.o.a., 3″ dia., pan 3⅜″ dia., tin.

11-11   DOUBLE KYAL LAMP

The Kyal lamps were nearly always provided with bails for suspension but could also be stood on their flat bases. They probably burned coal oil but some with copper spouts may have used fish or lard oil.

Description: 9¾″ h., 3¾″ dia., tin, American.

11-11

11-10   KYAL LAMP

Also known as a Cape Cod lamp, the Kyal is a crude modification of the Flemish spout lamp (Nos. 4-37, 4-38, p. 45), suitable for use only in shops where excessive smoking of a large wick could be tolerated. The main reservoir is supported in an outer cup with a trough to catch the drip from the spout.

Description: 7″ h., 4″ dia., tin, American.

11-12   EXTENDABLE CANDLEHOLDER

Many options were available to the user of this versatile shop light. Horizontal adjustment is provided by the jointed arm and vertical adjustment of the spring loaded yoke. The device itself could either be driven into the top of a bench or suspended from above, or from a nail in the wall, by the swivel loop. The socket with a drip pan is provided with a pushup to eject the stub.

Description: 15″ h.o.a., jointed rod extended from 5″ to 20″, socket 1″ dia., drip 2½″ dia., wrought iron, American.

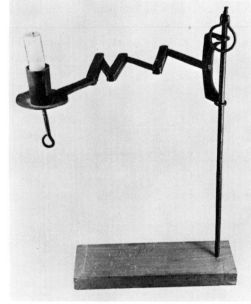

11-12

BAKER'S LAMP

11-13

11-13   BAKER'S OVEN LAMP

Sometimes called "witch" lamps, these cast iron lamps in the shape of a gravy boat with hinged cover (occasionally missing) and integral saucer were bakers' oven lamps. As in this example, the oven maker's name is sometimes cast in the cover.

Description: Base 6½″ l., font 3¼″ h., 5¼″ l., cast iron, marked "MIDDLEBY OVEN CO. BOSTON MASS", American.

11-15   WATER LENS

Sometimes called a lace maker's lamp, this blown glass globe when filled with water becomes a lens which was used in front of a candle or lamp to concentrate the light. The small glass ball cover was used to exclude dust and retard evaporation. Fish bowls of similar design but with large openings are sometimes confused with water lenses.

Description: 10″ h., base 4″ dia., globe 6″ dia., ball cover 3″ dia., blown glass, American.

11-16   MULTIPLE WATER LENS

A wooden frame supports four pendant water lenses around a central candle. A glass ring applied to the neck of the lens provided secure support by the leather strap. Water lenses were used by jewelers, shoemakers and other artisans as well as lace makers.

Description: Frame 11″ h., 7″ sq., base 7¾″ sq., walnut, lens dias. 3½″, 4½″, 5″, 5″., blown glass, American.

MECHANIC'S LAMP

11-14

11-14   MECHANIC'S LAMP

As in the case of miners' lamps, (p. 102), this cast iron mechanic's lamp was obviously made to take abuse. In addition to the wire loop for hanging, an applied strap is provided to allow for mounting in a wall bracket.

Description: 5¼″ l., cast iron, marked "STRENGTH DURABILITY NO. 5 WELLS SINGLE TORCH LAMP A.C.WELLS & CO. PATENTED", Welch.

LACEMAKER'S LAMPS

11-15   *11-16*

DOCTOR'S LAMP

11-17

11-17   LENS LAMP
A solid glass lens supported in a brass holder is used in this pewter lamp to concentrate the light. It is believed to have been a doctor's lamp.

Description: 5¼″ h., base 3¾″ dia., font 2″ dia., lens 2″ dia., pewter and brass.

11-19   ALCOHOL LAMP
Alcohol lamps in various forms were used by dentists, jewelers or other craftsmen as a source of heat, often for use with a blowpipe. In this example, the faceted font permits burning at a convenient angle; in other versions a spherical font is supported by a concave cup to provide ball and socket adjustability.

Description: 4½″ h.o.a., octagonal base, glass, marked "JUNE 26, 1883", American, ca. 19th century.

DENTIST'S OR JEWELER'S LAMP

11-19

LECTURER'S LAMP

11-18   LECTURER'S LAMP
A hinged poke bonnet cover controls and subdues the light from this spring loaded candleholder to illuminate a lecturer's notes, while a sliding shutter controls the beam from a small porthole on the back. A wire trigger projects from the base to ring a bell. Either the bell or small shuttered beam was used to signal a change of slides.

Description: 9½″ h., base 3″ sq., candleholder 3¾″ h., 1¾″ dia., porthole 1″ dia., tin, black japanned, American, ca. 1870.

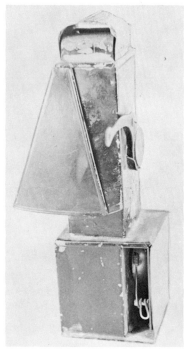

11-18

11-20   NURSERY LAMP
Based on the 1812 Howe patent, this nursery lamp provides several functions for the nursery or sickroom. A hinged door at the base controls the amount of light from a small two-tube whale oil lamp whose heat is used to warm food or liquids in a "double boiler" container formed by two nesting vessels supported by the top flange, and enclosed with a tin cover. Small perforations in the door and hooded vent holes at the top permit burning when the door is closed. A large handle on the back allows its use as a lantern when the door is open.

Description: 9¼″ h., 4⅜″ dia., top container 3¼″ h., 3⅜″ dia., lower container 4¼″ h., 3⅜″ dia., lamp 1¾″ h., 2⅝″ dia., tin, American, ca. 19th century.

NURSERY LAMP

11-20

WRITER'S LAMP

11-21

11-21

11-21 WRITER'S LAMP

Two requirements of the penman are fulfilled in this device. A small tin peg lamp with two-tube whale oil burner provides the illumination while the perforated tin base offers a socket for the peg lamp and a shaker housing for the blotting sand which also helped to stabilize the broad conical base.

Description: Far left: 4″ h.o.a., Center: lamp 2″ h., Far Right: base 4″ dia., tin, Pennsylvania.

11-22 SEWING LAMP STAND

Although not appreciably easing the severe visual task of sewing, this ingenious Betty lamp stand is a distinct convenience in organizing the tools of the needleworker. The broad base offers good stability and also serves as a lamp "tidy" (p. 120).

Description: Stand 8⅝″ h., base 8″ l., 7½″ w., tray 3¼″ l., 2¾″ w., wood, lamp 3¼″ dia., tin, American.

11-22

STUDENT'S LAMP

11-23 STUDENT'S LAMP

A counterpoised, vertical cylinder cardan reservoir balances an Argand lamp. Eye comfort with even distribution of light is assured by the ribbed green cased opal glass reflector shade. The lamp is rotationally and vertically adjustable on the tall central shaft.

Description: 20¼″ h., font 7½″ h., 3″ dia., nickel, shade 5½″ h., bottom 7″ dia., top 5″ dia., glass, burner stem marked "BERLIN", ca. late 19th century.

SEWER'S LAMP

11-23

FISHERMAN'S LAMP

PLASTERER'S LAMP

11-24

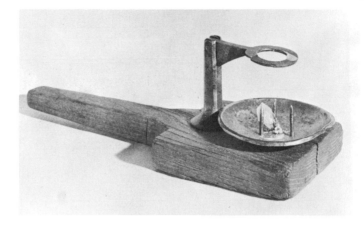

11-25

11-25   PLASTERER'S CANDLEHOLDER

This hand-held candleholder provided for the plasterer or painter, adequate light in close proximity to his demanding task. The candle, mounted in a pewter saveall saucer, is further supported by a bracket mounted pewter ring which encircles the candle.

Description: Holder 10″ l.o.a., 3⅞″ w., wood, saucer 3″ dia., shaft 2½″ h., pewter, English.

11-24   FISHERMAN'S CRESSET

Pine knots burning in cressets of this type were used by fishermen at night, and along piers for the benefit of dockworkers, (1-27), p. 8).

Description: 31″ l.o.a., 13¾″ w., rib span of each 6″, wrought iron, ca. 18th century.

11-26   FIREMAN'S LANTERN

Although lanterns were used for many general purposes, this example marked "Dietz King — Fire Dept." was made for that specific purpose, as evidenced by its heavy rustproof all brass construction, wire guard, and various methods of mounting on an engine. It was available with clear or red globe. The hinged wire guard provides access to the kerosene burner and chimney.

Description: 15″ h., 7″ dia., brass, marked "DIETZ KING — FIRE DEPT." "PATENTED AUG 27-07 MCH 24-91", American, ca. early 20th century.

FIREMAN'S LANTERN

11-26

BOILER INSPECTOR'S LAMP

11-27   BOILER TUBE LAMP

The slender boxlike reservoir and hooked wire bail allowed this boiler inspector's two-tube whale oil lamp to pass between the tubes of a steam boiler. An identical example is listed in a Boston ship chandler's catalog for 1913.

Description: 3½″ h., 4″ w., 1⅛″ d., galvanized, bail 8″ l. wire, American, ca. early 20th century.

11-27

POLICEMAN'S LAMP

11-28 WATCHMAN'S LANTERN

Dark lanterns equipped with pressed glass lenses appear in many forms and sizes, and with various auxiliary features. This example with two-tube whale oil lamp is unusual in having two lenses mounted at right angles which are hinged for access to the lamp.

Description: 7″ h., base 3″ dia., tin, japanned, lenses 2⅞″ dia., pressed glass, American, ca. 1840.

11-28

11-29

11-29 POLICEMAN'S LANTERNS

The large lantern on the right has an internal cylindrical shutter operated by an external knob. In the small lantern on the left, an inner cylinder acts as a shutter or provides white, red or green light by rotation of the ventilator cap to which it is attached.

Description: Left: 4½″ h.o.a., 2⅜″ dia., tin, brown japanned, glass lens 1⅞″ dia., red and green filter glasses, Right: 7½″ h., 3″ dia., tin, blue japanned marked "DIETZ POLICE", lens 3″ dia., pressed glass, American, ca. 19th century.

HOUSEKEEPER'S LAMP

11-30 LIGHTED DUSTPAN

There was no excuse for dirty floors in the home equipped with this lighted dustpan. The candleholder is mounted on an ingenious "handle" into which the toe of one's shoe could be inserted from any of three directions, to apply pressure.

Description: Tin - original label on back of pan "ILLUMINATED DUSTPAN MADE IN CONN. 1882", American, ca. 19th century.

11-31 STORE LAMP

A large wire bail supports a small smoke bell and large quilted tin reflector above this kerosene lamp. A generous two and a quarter inch cylindrical wick can be adjusted from below and the lamp itself can be removed from the frame for filling or cleaning by rotating the interlocking bottom bails. An added convenience is a fuel gauge on the top of the font.

Description: 33″ h.o.a., font 8″ dia., brass embossed marked "THE PITTSBURGH", fuel gauge marked "PAT OCT. 28 '90″, shade 20″ dia., tin, American, ca. 19th century.

STOREKEEPER'S LAMP

11-30

11-31

BENCH LIGHT

11-32

11-32   BENCH LIGHT

Bench workers in many crafts made use of inexpensive homemade candleholders such as this crude tin socket set in a block of wood.

Description: Base 3½″ 1., 2¾″ w., 1½″ thick, wood, socket 1″ h., tin, American.

ASTRONOMICAL LAMP

11-33

11-33   ASTRONOMICAL LANTERN

A row of four candles provides light to illuminate a transparency of the heavens that was inserted in the tin slides at the front of this lantern. Since the transparencies are usually missing, these devices are often mistaken for theater footlights.

Description: 9½″ h., 9¼″ w., 6″ d., tin black japanned, gilt decorations.

FOOTLIGHT

11-24   FOOTLIGHT

Six large wick tubes in this lamp, in combination with a polished tin reflector, provide the necessary amount of light for the stage of the town hall or theater. The reflector was permanently mounted to the floor while the lamp was removable for filling and trimming.

Description: Reflector 9″ h., 5¼″ w., lamp 3¼″ h., 4⅜″ dia., tin, American, ca. 19th century.

11-25   CHIMNEY TOP HEATER

This wire adapter fits the top of a kerosene lamp chimney and serves to hold for heating, either a curling iron or a small bowl of water. The wire adapters will securely fit most chimney sizes.

Description: Lamp 14″ h.o.a., base 4½″ dia., pressed glass, adjustable wire gallery 1½″ dia. to 4½″ dia., curling iron 8″ l.o.a., American, ca. early 20th century.

11-34

CURLING IRON

11-35

CHAPTER XII

FIRE MAKING DEVICES

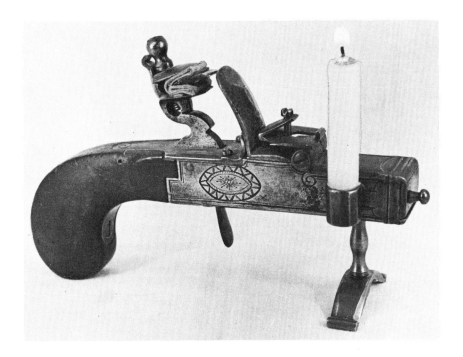

Since all of the early lighting devices depended upon combustion, the ability to create fire was one of man's most pressing needs. On a sunny day, the lens could harness the energy of the sun to ignite tinder, and from the early nineteenth century, various chemical means simplified the task. However, for many centuries, fire was obtained mainly by converting mechanical energy into heat by friction, compression or percussion. Percussion in the form of striking a steel with a piece of flint was the method used by most civilized cultures.

In most of these early methods a feeble spark was captured by some form of tinder, often consisting of charred linen. Slivers of wood tipped in sulphur, known as spunks, usually converted the glowing tinder to a useful flame.

The beginning of the nineteenth century introduced the chemical age of fire making which eventually replaced the mechanical means except for present day use in pocket lighters.

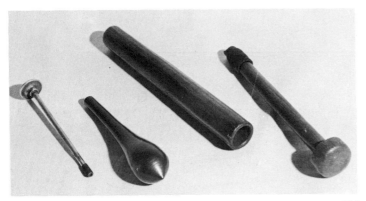

12-1

12-1   FIRE PISTONS

Although of primitive origin, the fire piston enjoyed limited use as a fire maker. Tinder is placed in a small recess at the end of the piston which when sharply struck compresses the air in the cylinder. The work of compression is converted into heat which ignites the tinder.

Description: Left: 5⅜" l., wood, maple, plunger 4¾" l., brass, Right: 7⅝" l., plunger 7" l., wood.

12-2

12-2   TINDERBOX

Tinderboxes take various forms. As in this early example, the minimum requirements were a striking steel and a compartment or two for the flint and tinder.

Description: 12" l., 4¼" w., 3½" h., wood, Danish.

12-3   TINDERBOX

Conventional in form, but unusual in material, is this wooden tinderbox with candleholder on the cover. Clearly shown is the tinder in the bottom of the box, the tin damping disc to extinguish the tinder and help keep it dry, and the flint and striker which were normally kept on top of the damper.

Description: 4⅝" dia., 3½" h.o.a., wood.

12-4   POCKET TINDERBOX

This small pocket box with corkscrew has the steel firmly affixed to the inside of the cover. The corkscrew is protected by a small tubular cover.

Description: 1¾" l., 1" w., 1" h., iron.

12-3

12-4

12-5   IVES PATENT TINDERBOX

A captive sliding lid covers three compartments, a small one near the wheel for tinder, the second one for the flint and the largest for small spunks. In use, the flint was held against the wheel which was revolved rapidly by pulling on a string wound around the axle.

Description: 3¾″ l., 1¼″ w., ⅞″ d., tin, wheel 1½″ dia., steel, marked on lid "IVES'S PATENT BRISTOL", English.

12-5

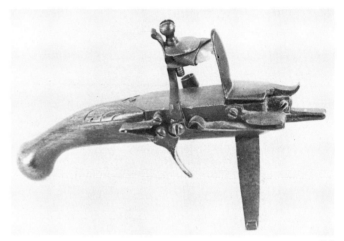

12-6   TINDER PISTOL

The familiar flint lock mechanism used in pistols and muskets appears in various forms of tinder pistols. The "pan" holds the tinder, and usually a small receptacle for spunks, and a socket for candle or taper is included.

Description: 8½″ l.o.a., 5½″ h.o.a., iron and wood, European.

12-6

12-7   CANE TINDER LIGHTER

The handle of this walking stick houses the three necessary components of the tinderbox — flint, striker and tinder.

Description: 36″ l., wood (ash).

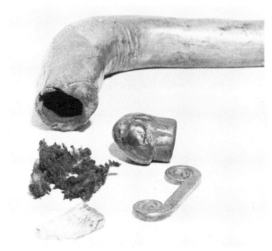

12-7

12-8   TINDER POUCHES

The "chuckmuck" or tinder pouch, worn from a waist belt, carried the flint and tinder, while the curved striking steel formed the bottom of the pouch.

Description: Left: 4½″ l., 2½″ w., leather with silver mountings, Right: 3½″ l., 2″ w., leather with brass trim, China or eastern Asia.

12-8

12-10 DOBEREINER LIGHTER

Probably the most sophisticated of the chemical lighters was the Dobereiner, invented by a German professor of chemistry in 1823. A built-in "computer" controlled the generation of hydrogen gas by the action of sulphuric acid on zinc. When a light was needed, a valve permitted the hydrogen to come in contact with a small platinum sponge which became incandescent and ignited the gas.

Description: 10½″ h., with metal top surmounted by figures of dwarf and dog, ca. 19th century.

12-9

12-9 REPEATING IGNITER

A patented English lighter in the form of a classical oil lamp conceals under a hinged cover, a wooden disc with ten small stearine candles each equipped with a friction primer. The disc rests on a turntable which is advanced mechanically by squeezing the two snake head handles, striking a light.

Description: 7″ l., 2½″ h., brass, stamped "PATENT B & AB", English, ca. 1867.

12-10

12-11 MATCHES

Among the first of the chemical lighters was the instantaneous light box (upper right) which housed a small blown bottle of asbestos saturated with sulphuric acid, and a supply of wooden matches tipped with chlorate of potash which ignited when dipped in the acid. "Friction" matches in various forms depended on chemistry for their success. To facilitate dipping and handling, block and comb matches (lower left) were made.

Description: Center: Stamped on cover with liberty bell and "1776", Clockwise: large block matches, "Portland Star Matches", small block matches, instantaneous lighter, 2¾″ h., 1¾″ w., blown bottle 1½″ h., tin brown japanned, "The Three Monkeys" safety match, Sweden, "Bryant and May's Braided Cigar Lights", England, "National Safety Matches", Sweden, large comb matches, "L. Baschiera E C", comb matches from Portland Star package.

12-12 SPILLS AND SPLINTS

Although not capable of creating fire, slivers or thin strips of wood called splints, and twisted tubes of paper or pine shavings called spills were used to transfer flame in lighting lamps, pipes and fires. The making of twisted paper spills provided a useful occupation for the very young or very old. Special planes were invented to simplify the production of wooden spills and splints.

Description: Paper and wood.

12-12

12-11

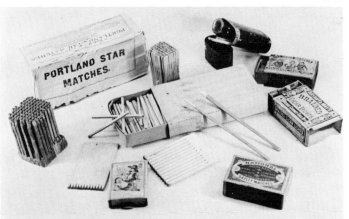

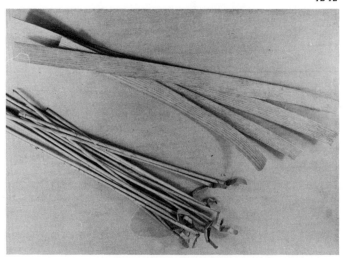

CHAPTER XIII

ACCESSORIES

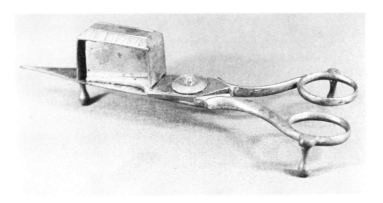

Although of themselves not lighting items, many accessories were needed to facilitate the preparation of candles and rushes, and for the maintenance and operation of all types of lighting. Each fuel presented its own problems.

Preparation of candles, whether by dipping or molding, was a slow task at best, and arrangements to make as many as possible at one time were a big help.

The storage of candles required special containers and their burning demanded constant attention, as well as protection from drafts to prevent guttering.

Oil lamps on the other hand required frequent filling and the wick adjustment was critical to avoid excessive smoking or extinguishing.

The wick adjustment problem was solved in the kerosene lamps but their tendency to smoke if not carefully adjusted necessitated chimney cleaners, and in pendant fixtures, the use of smoke bells.

Accessories range from very simple functional necessities to highly decorative specimens of folk art and ingenious examples of inventive talent.

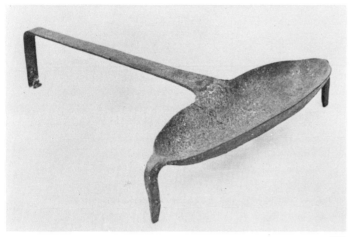

13-1

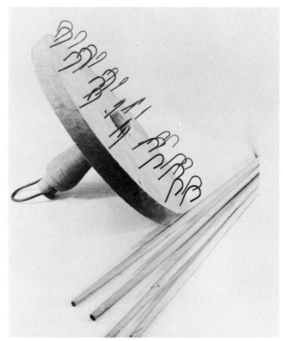

13-2

13-1　GRISSET

As simple and basic as the rushlight itself, is the grisset, a three-legged, handled canoe-shaped iron vessel, usually wrought, but occasionally cast, used near the fire to melt the tallow in which the peeled and dried rushes are dipped.

Description: 13½″ l., 4¼″ w., 2½″ h., handle 13¾″ l., 3⅜″ h., at rear, wrought iron, English, ca. 18th century.

13-2　CANDLE DIPS

Up to a dozen wicks could be suspended from the slender whittled candle rods (lower right) which were supported for drying between the backs of two chairs. The upper dipper (one of eight) is supported at the end of an eight-armed revolving wooden stand for drying. The circular shape was more efficient than rods when dipping in the usual round kettle.

Description: Left: 9⅞″ dia., wood, 31 wire hooks, Right: approx. 2′ long, wood, American.

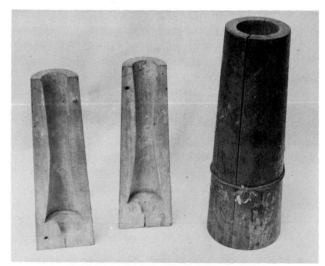

13-3

13-3　JAPANESE CANDLE MOLD

The traditional concave shape of Japanese candles requires a split mold for removal of the candle. The wick is stretched through a slot at the bottom to a small cross stick at the open end.

Description: 9½″ h., base 2¾″ dia., wood, Kyoto, Japan.

13-4　TIN CANDLE MOLDS

Tin molds were made in candle sizes from miniature tapers to large ceremonial candles. Molds were made with from one to one hundred and forty-four tubes. In the example at the right, the inverted tray on the bottom provides a base, and the tray on the top permits rapid pouring from a simple ladle. Although sometimes missing, a strap handle was usually provided for convenience in handling.

Description: Left: 10¾″ h.o.a., 4″ dia., tin, made 5-10″ candles, Right: 10¾″ h.o.a., 8¾″ w.o.a., 3⅞″ d., tin, made 12-9½″ candles, tin, American.

13-4

13-5

13-6

13-5   PEWTER CANDLE MOLD

Twelve pewter tubes mounted in a brass plate are framed in a mahogany stand. Small holes in the end plate support and locate the wire rod to which the wicks are fastened. As shown, the front side-piece is removable to facilitate removing the excess tallow after dipping and tying the wicks.

Description: 10¼″ l.o.a., 3¾″ w., 10⅛″ h., mahogany wood, marked "DYRE & RICHMOND NEW BEDFORD", 12 pewter tubes, American.

13-7   POTTERY CANDLE MOLD

Similar to the familiar pewter candle mold (13-5), this pine frame holds twenty-four redware candle tubes. Similar molds with glass tubes were also made.

Description: 24″ l.o.a., 9¼″ w., 14½″ h., pine, candle tubes pottery, American.

13-6   CANDLE MOLDING FRAME

This crude pine frame has holes to support sixteen single candle tubes with individual filling cups, which required time and care in pouring.

Description: 20½″ l., 10¼″ w., 20″ h., pine, candle tubes tin, American.

13-8   CANDLE MOLDING FRAME

Although using the conventional tin multiple tube mold, this simple frame provides a small degree of "automation" in the simultaneous threading of the wicks.

Description: 32″ h.o.a., 16½″ w., maple wood, candle mold top 9½″ l., 3¼″ w., tin, 16 candle tubes tin, American, ca. 19th century.

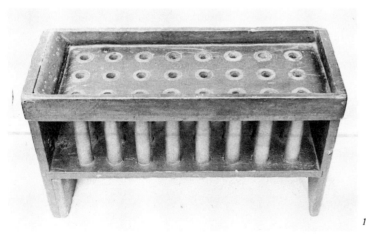

13-7

13-8

13-9

13-10

13-9 CANDLE BOX

Whether dipped or molded, tallow candles had to be stored safe from heat, fire and especially rodents. These cylindrical tin wall mounted boxes served this purpose.

Description: 13¾" l., 4⅝" dia., tin, American.

13-10 CANDLE EXTINGUISHERS

Candles could be quickly extinguished with a minimum of smoking by capping the flame with one of these small tin cones equipped with finger loop. Extinguishers were also made of other metals, as well as ceramics.

Description: Left: 3" h.o.a., base 1½" dia., Right: 2½" h., base 1" dia., tin, American, ca. 18th and 19th centuries.

13-11 SNUFFER AND HOLDER

The simple twisted wicks of the early candles were not fully consumed as the candle burned, resulting in a build-up of charred wick called snuff which caused the candle to gutter and smoke. A scissor-like contrivance (13-23, p. 121) usually with a small attached compart-

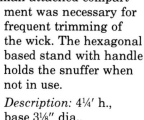

ment was necessary for frequent trimming of the wick. The hexagonal based stand with handle holds the snuffer when not in use.

Description: 4¼' h., base 3⅛" dia., hexagonal, brass, English, ca. 18th century.

13-11

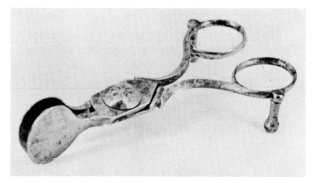

13-12

13-12 DOUTER

Unlike the snuffer which it slightly resembles, the douter provided a safe and clean way of pinching out a candle flame.

Description: 4⅛" l.o.a., pincer plates 1" dia., steel, English.

13-13

13-14

13-13 LAMP FILLER

Lamp fillers resembling small teapots were a great help in filling oil lamps through the small burner openings. The three essentials, a comfortable handle grip, a large opening for filling the lamp filler, and a slender curved pouring spout are beautifully incorporated in this free blown example.

Description: 3″ h., base 2⅝″ dia., top 3½″ dia., blown glass, American, ca. 1800-1825.

13-15 WICK PICK

The tubes of whale oil burners have small slots above the burner plate, and sometimes below, to permit adjustment of the wick by means of a wick pick, consisting of a small wire mounted in a handle, usually of wood, and stored in a matching base.

Description: Left: stand 2″ h., base 1½″ dia., Right: handle 1½″ l., pick 1½″ l., mahogany and steel, American, ca. 19th century.

13-14 LAMP FILLER

More commonly found is the tin lamp filler. This example has a hinged cover and a reinforced pouring spout. On some specimens, the handle is on the side.

Description: 5⅜″ h., base 4⅛″ dia., top 2¾″ dia., cover 1″ d., tin, American.

13-16 WICK PICKS

In addition to the conventional form (right), wick picks often appear in the form of whimsies as in the ivory egg held by the brass cup. Scrimshaw whimsy wick picks in the shape of miniature candlesticks with candles are also found, as well as those in the form of hand bells.

Description: Left: 1¾″ h., brass and ivory, Right: 3½″ h., base 1″ dia., wood, American.

13-15

13-16

13-17

13-18

13-17 WOOD BETTY LAMP STANDS

Turned wood stands or "tidies" raised the squat Betty lamp to a useful height when burned at a table, and at the same time protected the table from spilled fuel.

Description: Left: 6⅞" h., base 3" dia., top 2¾" dia., wood, Right: 7¾" h., base 3½" dia., top 3¼" dia., pine with traces of gilt, American.

13-18 POTTERY LAMP STAND

In Pennsylvania, redware with its typical forms of decoration was sometimes used for lamp tidies. Somewhat similar, and occasionally mistaken for the rare tidy, are redware stove supports which are about one half the height, and are sometimes found in sets of four.

Description: 5⅜" h., base 4¾" dia., top 3½" dia., redware, with salt glaze, Pennsylvania.

13-19

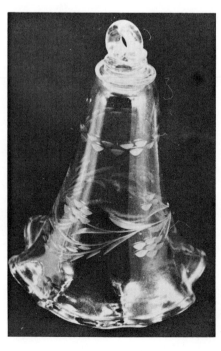

13-19 TIN BETTY LAMP STAND

Unlike the Portsmouth Betty (4-32, p. 43) with its integral base, and the Ipswich Betty (4-31, p. 43) with its individual stand, the tin tidy with a fluted tray was intended for use with any Betty lamp.

Description: 8⅜" h., base 6⅜" dia., top 5⅛" l., tin, American.

13-20 SMOKE BELL

Smoke bells, which could be easily cleaned, were made of glass or metal, and served to trap the soot before it could soil the ceiling. When made of opal glass or polished metal, they also served the added function of a reflector.

Description: 6¼" h.o.a., 4½" dia., blown glass, engraved, American, ca. 19th century.

13-20

13-21

13-22

13-21   MATCH SAFES

Matches required protection to keep them dry, and for safety. In these two examples, hinged covers protected the live matches while an open section in the back furnished a receptacle for burned matches which often saw further use as spills.

Description: Left: 3½″ h.o.a., base 3″ sq., box 2″ sq., sandpaper on front, tin, Right: 4″ h., base 2¾″ dia., holder 2¼″ dia., tin, red japanned with black decoration.

13-22   WALL MATCH TRAY

This crude tin match holder, made to hang on the wall, resembles the wall candle sconces (p.31).

Description: 7½″ h., tray 4¼″ l., 2″ w., 2″ h., tin, American.

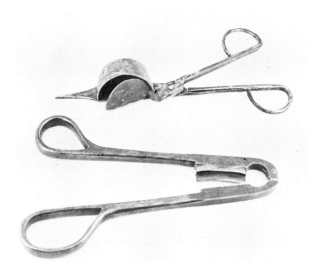

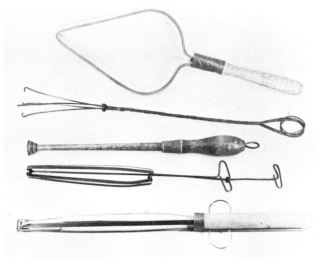

13-23

13-24

13-23   SNUFFER AND WICK
         TRIMMER

The snuffer (top) was used to snuff or trim the wicks of candles (13-11, p. 118), whereas the curved blade of the wick cutter (bottom) was used to trim the ribbon wick of a kerosene lamp to match the curve of the deflector cap. Many forms of kerosene wick trimmers were devised in the last half of the nineteenth century.

Description: Top 5⅝″ l.o.a., iron, Bottom: 6¾″ l., curved blade 1¼″ l., iron, anvil, brass, American, ca. 19th century.

13-24   CHIMNEY CLEANERS

The light output from a kerosene lamp was greatly reduced if the chimney got smoked. The chimney cleaner at the top consists of a thin spring steel ribbon covered with woven wicking, which when compressed, conforms to the shape of any chimney. The four bottom cleaners were designed to serve the dual purpose of cleaning chimneys or bottles by attaching a piece of cloth, and the cleaner next to the top was advertised for the additional feature of retrieving corks from empty bottles.

Description: Top: 13⅜″ l., spring steel ½″ w., wood handle, 2nd from top: 14¾″ l., steel wires, 3rd from top: 10¾″ l., wood with steel rod running through, forming spring handle, 4th from top: 12″ l., spring steel and wire, Bottom: 13″ l., wood and spring steel, American, ca. 19th and early 20th centuries.

13-25

13-25 HURRICANE GLOBE
Properly designed candles required no chimney for proper combustion but the hurricane globe was a useful accessory and prevented guttering when the candle burned in a draft.

Description: 16″ h., 8½″ dia., blown glass.

13-26

13-27 ADJUSTABLE LAMP STAND
Similar in design to the adjustable candle-stand (3-33, p. 25), this stand has no socket for candle or peg lamp. The two arms adjustable vertically and rotationally are slotted at the ends to grip the long hooks of Betty lamps, or a lamp could be hooked over the turned arms as shown.

Description: 24½″ h., base 7½″ dia., horizontal turning 12″ across, American.

13-26 TAPER JACK
The taper jack was designed to hold and burn the flexible coiled wax tapers used with sealing wax. This handsome example has an extinguisher attached to the holder by a small link chain.

Description: 6½″ h., sterling silver, marked "HOWARD 209 — STERLING 1884 — NEW YORK", American, ca. 19th century.

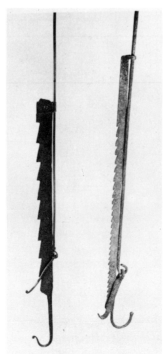

13-28 LAMP TRAMMELS
Resembling the heavier fireplace trammel, but much more delicate in design, these sawtooth lamp trammels offered a wide range of vertical adjustment, similar to trammel candleholders (3-47, p. 29), but with the advantage of accommodating any lighting device designed for suspension.

Description: Left: 18″ l., suspension to 31″, Right: 19″ l., suspension to 38″ l., wrought iron, ca. 18th century.

13-28

13-27

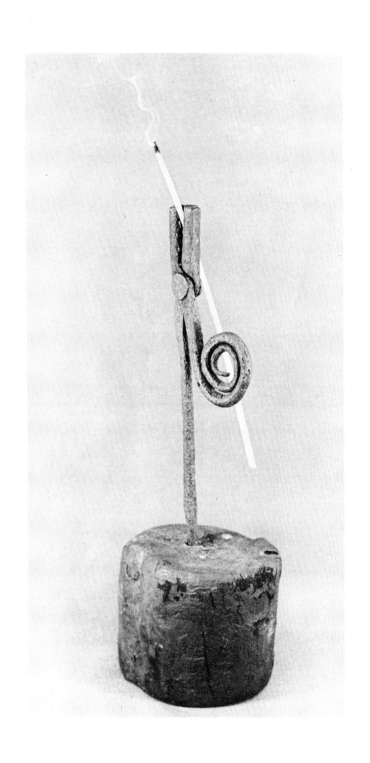

THE END

BIBLIOGRAPHY

BAILEY, DONALD M. *Greek and Roman Pottery Lamps.* England: (Pub. by Trustees of The British Museum), Eyre and Spottiswoode Ltd., at Grosvenor Press, Portsmouth, 1963.

BERNTSEN, ARNSTEIN. *Ly Sog Lysstell, Gjennom 1000 Ar.* Oslo, Norway: Gyldendal Norsk Forlag, 1965.

†BUTLER, JOSEPH T. *Candleholders in America 1650-1900.* New York: Crown Publishers, Inc., 1967.

CHRISTY, MILLER. *The Bryant and May Museum of Fire-Making Appliances: Catalogue of the Exhibits.* London: Bryant & May Ltd., 1926. Supplement, 1928.

COLLINS, HERBERT R. "Political Campaign Torches," *U. S. Natl. Museum Bulletin* No. 241, 1964.

D'ALLEMAGNE, HENRY-RENE. *Histoire du luminaire depuis l'epoque Romaine jusqu'au XIX siecle.* Paris: Alphonse Picard, 1891.

†DARBEE, HERBERT C. "A Glossary of Old Lamps" *History News,* American Assoc. for State and Local History, Tech. Leaflet 30, Nashville, Tenn., 1965.

FARADAY, MICHAEL. *The Chemical History Of a Candle.* New York: Harper & Bros., 1878.

FREEMAN, LARRY. *New Light on Old Lamps.* Watkins Glen, N. Y.: Century House, 1968.

GOULD, MR. AND MRS. G. GLEN. *Period Lighting Fixtures.* New York: Dodd, Mead & Co., 1928.

†HAYWARD, ARTHUR H. *Colonial Lighting.* 3rd enlarged ed. with Intro. and Supplement "Colonial Chandeliers" by James R. Marsh. New York: Dover Publications Inc., 1962.

†HEBARD, HELEN BRIGHAM. *Early Lighting in New England 1620-1861.* Rutland, Vt.: Charles E. Tuttle Co., 1964.

HOUGH, WALTER. "Collection of Heating and Lighting Utensils in the U. S. Natl. Museum," Smithsonian Inst., *U. S. Natl. Mus. Bull.* 141, 1928.

———. "Fire As An Agent in Human Culture" *U. S. Natl. Museum Bull. 139, 1926.*

———. "Fire-Making Apparatus in the U. S. Natl. Museum", No. 2735 *(From the proceedings of the U. S. Natl. Museum,* Vol. 73, Art. 14), 1928.

———. *The Story of Fire.* New York: Doubleday, Doran & Co., 1928.

ILIN, M. *Turning Night Into Day: The Story of Lighting.* (Translated from the Russian by Beatrice Kinkead). Philadelphia: London: J. P. Lippincott Co., 1936.

LUCKIESH, M. *Artificial Light.* New York: The Century Co., 1920.

———. *Torch Of Civilization.* New York: G. B. Putnam's Sons, 1940.

MACSWIGGAN, AMELIA E. *Fairy Lamps.* New York: Fountainhead Pub. Inc., 1962.

MERCER, HENRY C. "Light and Fire Making," *Contributions to American History, Bucks County Hist. Soc.* No. 4: Doylestown, Pa., 1898.

†O'DEA, WILLIAM T. *The Social History of Lighting.* London: Routledge and Kegan Paul, 1958.

———. "A Short History of Lighting" *Science Museum.* London: Her Majesty's Staty. Office, 1958.

———. "Making Fire", *Science Museum illus. booklet,* London: Her Majesty's Staty. Office, 1964.

PERRY, DAVID H. "Out Of Darkness" *Rochester Museum and Science Center,* Rochester, N. Y., 1969.

†ROBINS, F. W. *The Story Of The Lamp.* (Reprinted). Bath, England: Pitman Press, 1970.

ROY, L. M. A. *The Candle Book.* Brattleboro, Vt.: Stephen Daye Press, 1938.

†RUSSELL, LORIS S. *A Heritage Of Light.* Toronto, Canada: University of Toronto Press, 1968.

———. "Lighting The Pioneer Ontario Home" *Royal Ontario Museum.* Toronto: 1966.

SMITH, FRANK R. & RUTH E. *Miniature Lamps.* New York and Toronto: Thomas Nelson & Sons, 1968.

THOMAS, W. G. MACKAY. *English Candlesticks Before 1600.* London: Metropolitan Stationary Co., Ltd., 1954.

†THWING, LEROY L. *Flickering Flames*. Rutland, Vt.: Charles E. Tuttle Co., 1958.

———. *Old Lamps of Central Europe.* Edited and translated from the German *Das Beleuchtungswesen* by Ladislaus Edler Von Benesch (1905). Rutland, Vt.: Charles E. Tuttle Co., 1962.

TIDY, CHARLES M. *The Story of a Tinder-Box.* New York: E. & J. B. Young & Co., 1897.

WADSWORTH ATHENEUM. "Let There Be Light" *Catalogue of Exhibition,* with introduction by William T. O'Dea, Hartford, Conn., 1964.

†WATKINS, C. MALCOLM. "Artificial Lighting in American 1830-1860". *U. S. Natl. Museum, (From Smithsonian Report for 1951),* Smithsonian Inst. Publ. 4080, 1952.

† Suggested for a basic lighting library.

INDEX